Praise For
The Dark Side of Disney

"*The Dark Side of Disney* shines a light into the roachy shadows of Walt Disney World. With 33 years of experience storming the gates of the Magic Castle, Leonard Kinsey has explored every possible option for a low-cost Disney vacation ranging from the immoral to the downright illegal. Packed with all the tips that Disney was hoping you wouldn't discover, like free parking and bottomless beverage scams, this book also teaches you how to get free airline drink tickets and bar/pool hop around the high end Disney resorts like Hollywood glitterati.

Ever wanted to know where to have uninterrupted coitus on property? Kinsey points the way. Where to score weed? Keep reading. Kinsey charges to the roof of The Contemporary and spelunks into The Utilidors to bring you the finest nuances of an underground Disney vacation.

Pack the trunks and leave the kids at Grandma's because *The Dark Side* is about to make your next Disney vacation the best one ever!"

-Chris Mitchell, author *Cast Member Confidential*

The Dark Side of Disney

Leonard Kinsey

BAMBOO FOREST
PUBLISHING

IBN: 978-0615506135

Published by Bamboo Forest Publishing
First Printing: August, 2011

Visit us Online at:
www.darksideofdisney.com

Table of Contents

Having Fun Without Spending a Dime

Monorail Bar Crawl
Free Boat Rides
Pool Hopping

Sex

At the Resorts
In the Parks
How to Find Someone to Have Sex With
Alternative Lifestyle Activities
The Last Resort (Escort Services)

Drugs

Where to Score?
How to Safely Get High in the Parks
Top 5 Best and Worst Places to Get High

Rock N' Roll

Rock Venues On-Site
Food and Wine "Eat to the Beat"
Nightly Epcot Acts

Front of the Line With a Wheelchair

Taking the Resort Monorail

FastPass Scams

Refillable Mugs

Pin Trading Scams

Bed Bugs and Other Creepy Crawlies

Introduction

*Y*ou hold in your hands the key to a Walt Disney World vacation unlike any other. Regardless of how much money you make, or how many times you've already been to the parks, or how much you totally fucking hate "It's a Small World", this book will show you a side of WDW that is unique, exciting, and absolutely, unequivocally, NOT authorized by Disney. Within these pages you'll not only find tips on the best deals for airfare, food, and lodging (tips banned from official guidebooks and even most unofficial websites and messageboards), but diatribes on the best places in the parks to have sex, do drugs, and see a gritty rock show, complete with women throwing their underwear on the stage. You'll hear from people who have jumped out of ride vehicles and explored off-limits areas, who have swam across alligator infested lakes to see the ruins of abandoned parks, and who have dodged security to traverse the mysterious tunnels underneath The Magic Kingdom. You'll find tips on avoiding not only the dangerous Florida wildlife, but also the dangerous scammers who swarm Orlando like mosquitoes, just waiting to weasel you out of your hard-earned cash with their counterfeit merchandise, illegal ticket resales, and hard-sell timeshare presentations.

I've gathered all of this information over 33 years of visiting Walt Disney World, fortunate enough to have been born in Clearwater, Florida, and to have had a mother who shared my Disney obsession. Even though we were decidedly lower-middle class, she worked hard so she could spoil me and my sister with "Four Season Salute Passes" every Christmas, allowing us to visit as often as we wanted during non-peak months. And visit often we did, making the two-hour drive to Orlando at least once a month, often staying overnight at the (as of that time) only affordable on-site lodging, The Caribbean Beach Resort.

I don't remember my first visit to The Magic Kingdom; I was only 16 months old, but I have seen the pictures and I look pretty fucking thrilled. However, I do distinctly remember my excitement when, in 1st grade, I found a promotional book for EPCOT Center that had been sent to my teacher and unceremoniously shoved into the community bookshelf, just waiting to get torn apart by my snot-nosed classmates. I promptly stole the book, and spent hours poring over the concept art, genuinely believing that this park would be the best place in the world. Luckily, my mother was the manager of a day care, and since EPCOT at that time was touting itself as learning center (something that has long since been abandoned), she was able to snag opening-day tickets after much pleading on my part. I remember that first visit to EPCOT, in awe at seeing the concept art I'd been studying come to life, and having my mind blown by the architecture, animatronics, and a totally kick-ass vision of the future. I fell in love with computers that day, and became a nerd for life. And I remember knowing with all my heart that, yes, this actually was the best place in the world. I still believe that to this day.

Because, and I want to make this clear, I LOVE WALT DISNEY WORLD! I know the parks like the back of my hand, and I could walk through them blindfolded, guided only by the lovely scents and sounds meticulously crafted by those brilliant Imagineers. There's a comfort in being there, like returning home. Except that when I actually do go back to my childhood home, everything has changed. They tore down the forests I used to play in, paved over the pond I fished in, and repainted my house bright pink. Nothing is familiar, nothing is comforting. But for the most part Walt Disney World stays the same, always providing the sights, sounds, and smells that immediately bring me back to a more carefree time in life. And when it doesn't stay the same, when the company fucks up, like when Horizons was torn down, at least I'm not the only one grieving; there are thousands of others across the world to commiserate with.

It should also be known that I'm a huge fan of Walt Disney himself, devouring any and all documentaries and biographies I can find about the man. I'm consistently finding inspiration in his life story, his determination against all odds, and his visionary, forward-thinking outlook not only on family entertainment, but on the human experience and the future of mankind. From viewing his final EPCOT film and reading his final interviews, it seems as if he was ready to completely redefine city living, in a real paradigm-shifting game-changing sort of way. I believe he could have done it, too, could have pulled it all together just as he'd achieved the impossible countless times before, and I feel for Roy Disney and Card Walker for having to pick up the pieces, desperately trying to make something out of them without their leader at the helm. It's a shame that what we ended up with in Kissimmee is a Walt Disney World only half-finished, only half-perfect. But half of perfection is still pretty fucking awesome.

So, no, I don't have some big grudge against Disney, and the purpose of this book is not to try to destroy the company or dissuade people from visiting their theme parks. Quite the opposite, in fact; I wrote this book hoping to provide a definitive answer the assholes who always ask, "You're going there again?! Why do you keep going to that kiddie place?" and then shake their heads while they head back to Aspen or Vegas for the 80th time for their "adult" vacations.

Honestly, I have to admit that I once thought this way, too. No matter how big of a fan-boy I was, by age 16 or so I was bored as hell with WDW, having already visited the (at that time) three parks over 100 times. So I started experimenting with "alternative activities" every time I got dragged back there, and began to gather some of the tips in this book. This really came to a head when I was in college, running the campus television station, and desperate for content to fill our 24/7 programming roster. I was going home for Spring Break, and had a brilliant idea: I'd go to WDW and film all of the crazy shit my friends and I had been doing there for years, and then broadcast it on the station as a multi-part documentary. And thus was born the first incarnation of THE DARK SIDE OF DISNEY, complete with a CGI Tinkerbell lookalike shoving her magic wand into some guy's ass in the opening credits (meant as an homage to the Tinkerbell in the Disney Sunday Movies intro). I received no feedback, and to be honest, even though it was broadcast to every dorm on campus at least 200 times, I'm still not sure anyone watched the damn thing. I mean, what college kid in his right mind gives a shit about Walt Disney World? Most of them only cared about sex, drugs, and rock and roll... which I did, too, just as long as they took place at WDW. And I'm only half joking, unfortunately.... I didn't get laid much in college!

Regardless, as much as I love Walt Disney World, if it weren't for the tips in this book, I wouldn't go back nearly as often as I do. There are only so many times you can ride Space Mountain before it starts getting boring, but riding it on 'shrooms while getting a handjob is a totally different experience! So what we have here are at least 20 years of me pushing the limits just a little bit each time I returned to WDW, always trying to have a unique and exciting vacation. And now I'm releasing those tips to all of you, hoping you'll give WDW another chance, and maybe recapture some of that wonder, and yes, magic, you had for the place when you were a kid. Because we're all kids at heart, still desiring that same of thrill of newness that every day seemed to bring in those early years, but always knowing the comfort and safety of home lay just a few steps away. Well, Walt Disney World is home to everyone, young and old, and despite the thick skin we grow as we reach adulthood, I truly believe it's still the best place around to recapture the thrill and wonder of youth. Add in sex, booze, and other such debauchery, and that makes for one hell of a fun vacation.

1

Disney World,
Done Dirt Cheap

Let's face it, a vacation at Walt Disney World is almost prohibitively expensive. Between plane tickets, hotel rooms, park tickets, souvenirs, and food, expenses get out of hand quickly. A lot of people save up for years for a Disney vacation, and will still have to stay at the Value resorts (or ugh, off site), don't get Park Hoppers, and have to eat only at the quick-service restaurants. Souvenirs? Forget it. How often have you heard a parent at Mouse Gears yelling at their crying kid, "I'm not paying $30 for some stupid mouse ears!"

Let it be known that this author is certainly not rolling in the dough. Quite the opposite, in fact. But when I do WDW, I like to do it in style, and since I go at least once a year, that means I have to find ways to save a butt-ton of cash. So over the years I've devised numerous ways to cut costs, and to be honest, some of them are distasteful and will not appeal to the general populace. But if you want to do WDW on the ULTRA-CHEAP, read on!

GETTING THERE

Driving is For Suckers:

There's no way around this one; you have to get to the parks somehow. I absolutely do not recommend driving if you're more than 4 hours away. You're basically wasting two days of your vacation in the car, and that is not a magical way to spend the beginning and the end of your vacation. Plus, with gas prices what they are now, it's simply not economical.

My co-worker Matt told me what is probably the penultimate Disney road trip horror story. "We planned to drive down in our minivan from Baltimore," he starts. "It's an 18 hour drive, and my wife and I were just going to do it straight through. So we woke up at 4AM, shoved the kids, 12 and 8, into the minivan and were off.

"Everything was fine until we stopped at *South of the Border* in South Carolina. We went there for gas and the kids ran into the store whooping and hollering like they thought this was Disney. I'm yelling at my wife to get them back in the car, so she runs in after them. Then I stand there like an idiot for 10 minutes after I finish pumping the gas and they never come back out! So I have to go into that shithole and literally pull them out of the place. I fucking hate that tourist trap!

"Anyway, I finally get them of there after spending way too much money on cheap trinkets, and we're a few miles away when it starts pouring down rain. Like, that crazy rain where you can't see a foot in front of your car.

"At this point my 8 year old son decides it's the perfect time to start shooting off a bunch of party poppers he pocketed at *South of the Border.* You know, those little things where you pull the string and they explode and a bunch of shit comes flying out? Well he rips through what seems like five or six of them in about two seconds and is laughing like a maniac. My 12 year old daughter starts yelling, "My eyes are burned!" so my wife freaks out and is screaming at me to pull over, and I don't know what the fuck is going on so I'm in the middle lane swerving around and freaking out. I end up swiping a car in the right lane while I'm desperately trying to get over to the median. That car skids out, gets hit by another car, which gets hit by another car, and so on.

"We finally stop in the median and I look back and see almost a dozen cars stacked up on I95. There's fire, there's a lady stumbling out of her car with blood pouring out of her face, and the fucking rain has turned to hail and there are bloody people getting pelted and just falling on the ground screaming.

"It was the most horrendous thing I've ever witnessed in my life. The 12 year old is still in therapy because of it. We never did get to Disney. That was easily the worst vacation I've ever been on, and probably the worst experience of my life."

Moral of the story: take a plane!

Southwest Is Best:

The airline of choice for getting to WDW is Southwest Airlines. At the time of this writing, Southwest is merging with AirTran. What this means to WDW vacationers is probably that you're going to get cheaper flights from a wider variety of locations. Every year I compare the costs of Southwest's flights vs. AirTran (and Delta, American, and all the others) and Southwest always comes out ahead. Don't forget to factor in baggage fees when you're doing such a comparison.

Southwest is great because they don't charge said baggage fees, their fares are published far in advance, and their schedules stay consistent (as opposed to AirTran, who changes their flight schedules so often that it seems like there must be a crazy monkey throwing darts at a scheduling dartboard every month). And they've recently become a part of the Disney Magical Express program, which means that a) you don't need to rent a car because Disney will bus you to your resort from MCO (i.e., they'll take you hostage for the length of your stay) and b) your luggage will be delivered to your room when you arrive and will be taken to the

Disney's Magical Express luggage tag

airport for you when you depart. I've only had good experiences with Southwest and with the DME program.

For better or for worse, this is one of those occasions where it pays to plan ahead. Southwest publishes their fares by grades, and the cheapest of these grades are the "Wanna Get Away" fares. Unfortunately, these go quickly and once they're sold out you're left with the non-cheap "Anytime" and "Business Select" options. Southwest generally publishes their flights 180 days in advance, so it would behoove you to check them on the day that your fares are published and lock in the lowest rate.

"But what if the rates go lower?" you ask. Well, inquisitive reader, another great thing about Southwest is that they'll allow you to cancel your reservations at any time and get a credit. Which means that if you find a cheaper fare between when you booked your flight and the day of your vacation, you simply call them up, cancel the old flight, and purchase the new one. You don't get any cash back, but you will have credit in your account which you can use the next time you go to WDW (which, if you're reading this book will probably be pretty soon).

Another perk about booking Southwest is that they often offer discount codes, especially for flights to Florida. So even if you've already booked your flights, if you get a code in your email you can cancel your current reservation and rebook with the code. This author recently saved $25 each way with such a code! That was a big discount, and one which simply cannot be beat by any other airline out there. If you weren't offered a code via email, you can often get one by begging in threads on the "Budget Board" on disboards.com, or by buying one on eBay for pennies on the dollar.

Driving Drunk on The Disney Magical Express

Personally, I think the best part about flying Southwest is the drink tickets. Yes, that's right, DRINK TICKETS! You hand the stewardess this little piece of paper, and in return they give you an alcoholic beverage. Cash be damned! "Wait a minute," you say, "I don't have these drink tickets. I've never been offered these drink tickets. How do I acquire these mythical drink tickets?!" It's true, us mere mortals cannot get drink tickets on our own. They're only given out to people who fly a lot. In other words, people who have a lot of money or work for a company that has a lot of money and can fly them around everywhere, allowing them to rack up frequent flyer miles and boatloads of free drinks.

But despair not, faithful reader, there is a way for us plebeians to get

The Disney Magical Express bus, aka The Disney Drunk Taxi

the free drinkage: eBay! Go to ebay.com, type in Southwest drink tickets, and behold the splendor of the free market. You see, some people are teetotalers, which means they don't drink, which blows my mind. But it works out great for us lushes, because these snooty non-drinkers (like the girl sitting next to you on the plane who orders a Bloody Mary mix WITH NO VODKA) sell their SW drink tickets on eBay for dirt cheap! You can essentially buy $100 worth of drinks for $20, meaning you're getting an ice-cold Heineken or gin and tonic for a buck. I can think of no better way to start a vacation than getting loaded on discounted airline booze, knowing that you don't have to drive anywhere because Disney is going to pick you up from the airport in their nice air-conditioned bus.

Update: Southwest has changed their drink ticket policy so that Business Select tickets can only be used for a particular flight, and Rapid Rewards tickets are only valid for a year.

And drink tickets aren't the only way to get loaded on your flight into Florida. Most people dread layovers, because they're sitting in a crowded airport twiddling their thumbs, just waiting for time to pass so they can get on with their vacation. But not me. Nope, I actually schedule LONGER layovers on purpose!

Southwest's drink coupons, being used on the plane!

"WTF?!" you exclaim. "Why would any fool want a longer layover?!"

Well, the explanation is simple: I have passes to the ultra-exclusive airline VIP lounges, where the food is free and the drinks are plentiful... and free.

Again, eBay to the rescue! You can search for day passes to any of the major airlines' VIP lounges on eBay and bid on them for dirt cheap. I've been able to get them for as little as $12 for a day pass, meaning you could theoretically hit three lounges in one day (one at your departure point, one at the layover, and one in MCO). Just go to the individual airlines' websites and verify that they do have a lounge at your layover location. You don't have to be flying on that airline to take advantage of this, and at most airports the longest walk will be less than 20 minutes from your gate to the lounge furthest away.

Personally, I LOVE the Delta Sky Club, especially the one at O'Hare. Self-serve bar with top-shelf liquors, Heineken on draft, hummus, pretzels, cookies, cheese, and little packs of Nutella are just some of the highlights. I highly recommend bringing a backpack and loading up on snacks; the lounge is so huge and understaffed that there's no way they'll know you're taking food out. I'd also highly recommend getting completely blasted while there. Remember, you don't have to drive, Disney is doing all the driving for you!

STAYING THERE

Off-Site Horror Story:

The first rule about staying off site is: You do not stay off site. The second rule about staying off site is: YOU DO NOT STAY OFF SITE! Seriously. You might think you're being all smart saving a few bucks by staying at one of the myriad of hotels outside of WDW property, but trust me, you're doing it at the expense of a nice, relaxing vacation.

I have a friend, Michelle, who told me an admittedly outrageous version of what seems to be a fairly common tale of off-site hotels. Turns out Michelle and her family had stayed at a hotel marketing itself as being "just outside the main gate", which really meant, "a long ass way from any of the parks."

"We took a town car from the airport and got to the hotel at about 11AM," she starts. "We thought we'd see Cinderella's Castle from our window they way they described it, but the driver said the parks were at least five miles away. That's apparently still considered 'main gate'?

"The lobby was packed with cranky families and it took us almost an hour to check into our room. The people at the front desk were just plain mean. When we got to our room it stunk like cigarettes and mildew, and there was a bloody sock on the floor! Yes, a bloody sock! So we went to the front desk to get switched to another room, which took another 45 minutes. Fine, I guess maybe that sort of thing happens even at the best hotels. But then we got unpacked and went down to the lobby to catch the bus to the parks, and it turns out there is no bus! Well, there is, but it's not coming anytime soon. Apparently they only do drop-offs from 8AM-11AM, and then pick-ups from 7PM-11PM, and it only goes to The Magic Kingdom, so we'd have to take another bus to get over to any of the other parks!

"Obviously this was not what was advertised on their website. We were not happy about it, and tried to take it up with this squirrelly little manager, but he was completely unsympathetic, and pretty much yelled at us for not reading the fine print when we booked our reservations. I was crying, my daughter was crying, and Chris, my husband, was pissed; I thought he was going to punch somebody!

"I was so fed up that I called Disney Reservations, told the Cast Member, Missy, what had happened, and even though they were technically sold out for the week, Missy got us a room at All Stars. Surprisingly, it didn't really even cost much more than this dirtbag hotel we were staying at. Missy was so nice and understanding, I just couldn't believe it, and I was so happy and so grateful that we were both crying by the time I got off the phone!

"Chris had been watching me the whole time and thought Disney was being mean to me, too, but I told him how Missy had hooked us up. We had a group hug and Chris told the hotel manager where he could shove it. Then the manager started yelling about how we'd still get billed for the whole week, and how he'd say we destroyed our room and we'd get charged thousands of dollars! Chris was so happy about getting the hell out of there that he just laughed and gave the manager the finger, but then the manager actually charged at Chris right in front of all of these people in the lobby! Luckily a few of the other staff members held him back, but wow! Can you believe the guy actually tried to attack my husband? You wouldn't see that happen at Disney!

"In the end it all turned out great. We had a wonderful vacation, ended up LOVING All Stars, and came away with a hilarious story to tell. On top of that, our credit card company (American Express – woo!) took care of us and reversed the charges at the shitty hotel.

"Lesson learned, though. Sure, the off-site place was cheap," admits Michelle, "but from now it's only Disney Resorts for us. They went out of their way to take care of our terrible situation, the staff was all really friendly, the rooms were clean, the food court was wonderful, and the busses ran every 15 minutes. It was well worth the few extra dollars we spent. And I sent Disney a letter saying how great Missy was to us. I hope she gets a promotion!

"When we got back home we checked the reviews for the shithole place on TripAdvisor.com, which admittedly, we should have done beforehand. Turns out there were a bunch of stories just like ours, most with not so happy endings. We also noticed that a lot of the reviews for other cheapo 'main gate' hotels were just as awful. So make sure you tell everyone to stay on Disney property!"

Listen to Michelle!

A Deluxe for Less Than a Value?:

Disney offers many, many discounts throughout the year on rooms, most combined into packages with park tickets, gift cards to be used in the parks, and Free Dining (which will be discussed in the cheap food section). And these are good deals, definitely nothing to scoff at.

But you can find details on those packages anywhere, so there's no point in wasting space going over them here. What I'd like to do is to fill you in on the secret of how you can get rooms at the Deluxe Resorts for the same price as the Value Resorts: it's called "Renting Points". This isn't something Disney wants you to know about, and to be honest it's not entirely kosher. But people do it all the time, and Disney lets it slide, no questions asked.

Renting points is specific to the Disney Vacation Club Resorts, which is Disney's fancy name for a timeshare. "Owners" buy a certain number of "points" that they get each year for the life of the contract (for example, The Boardwalk Villas contracts expire in 2042). They pay a certain amount in yearly maintenance fees, depending on the number of points they own. It's not exactly an inexpensive commitment; normal contracts run in the 10s of thousands, and yearly maintenance fees can be thousands of dollars.

Each owner buys into a home resort on Disney property, many of which are a sub-section of a Deluxe resort (such as Bay Lake Towers at The Contemporary or Kidani Village at Animal Kingdom Lodge). These resorts all offer deluxe amenities, from "suites" that have kitchenettes, to 1-2-bedrooms that have full kitchens, Jacuzzis, and laundry machines. These are definitely a step above the Value or Moderate resorts, and similar accommodations at the Deluxe resorts start at $300/night (if you're lucky!).

When I went on vacation with my family as a kid, we always stayed at the Value and Moderate resorts, because that's all we could afford. DVC didn't even exist yet. I'm certainly not going to deny that my family had some amazing vacations and absolutely loved those resorts, and I'm not trying to tell you that you won't have a magical vacation at the Values or Moderates. I still have a major soft spot in my heart for The Caribbean Beach. But I have to say, once you go Deluxe, you'll never want to go back. And why not, when you can get them for the same price, if not cheaper, than a Value? Staying at The Boardwalk or The Beach Club and being able to walk to Epcot during The Food and Wine Festival just can't be beat, and have you SEEN Stormalong Bay, the "pool" at The Yacht and Beach Club? Calling it a pool is like calling The Grand Canyon a ditch! Or how about waking up in a room at Kidani Village, opening your blinds, and seeing a giraffe staring back at you? While the cheaper resorts are great, they simply don't offer those sorts of otherworldly experiences, the kind that make memories you brag to your friends about for years.

Now for the boring details. Stay with me here – this is tedious but it's important to understand DVC in order to fully take advantage of it. The owners of these timeshares, depending on the time of year and the type of room they want, use a certain number of points to reserve their room; more points are required for bigger rooms during busier times of the year. The owners buy a specific number of points to use each year at a particular resort, and they can also use those points for other resorts (although you can book 11 months out at your home resort, as opposed to 7 months at other resorts). So what happens is that people find that they have points left over at the end of the year, and although Disney allows you to bank points into the next year, if you still don't use them, you lose them.

When people have extra points that they know they won't be able to use, instead of just letting them expire they can "rent" the points. In short, they're booking a reservation for someone else. This can work one of two ways: 1) you either contact a DVC owner and have them check on resort availability, hoping that the resort you want is open on the dates you want it, or 2) the owner already has a reservation they can't use, and it just happens to be during the dates you want at the resort of your choice.

The first way of doing it works best if you can plan 11 months in advance, which is the earliest owners can book at their home resorts. After that the more in demand resorts get booked up quickly, and you're usually left with the biggest DVC resorts, Old Key West or Saratoga Springs (both of which are very nice, by the way). The best way to book with this method is to go to the DVC Rent/Trade subforum at disboards.com and start contacting people who say they have points for rent. They'll check availability for you, and then book the reservation in your name if something is open.

However, if it's less than 11 months out and you have a particular resort you want to book, you're probably better off finding someone who has a reservation they can't use. The best way to do this is to post a "Reservation

Wanted" thread at MouseOwners.com. Unfortunately Disboards no longer allows people to post "Reservation Wanted" threads more than one month in advance of the reservation date, which makes advance planning impossible. While MouseOwners doesn't get the level of traffic that Disboards does, it's still your best bet, and I've only had good luck with owners there.

In either scenario, once you find someone who will rent a reservation, you'll need to pay them for it. Right now the going rate is $9-$10/point, which means that for a prime week in a studio at The Boardwalk Villas in October (during the Food and Wine Festival) you'll be paying between $609-$670 for the week, which makes it at most $112/night total!!! Take that Value Resorts! You can calculate the points and thus the total cost for the length of your stay by using a DVC Point Calculator. There's a good one at www.wdwinfo.com/resort/dvcpoint.cfm

Most owners take PayPal as their preferred method of payment, and most will usually tack on a 3% charge to offset the PayPal fees. Although this costs you a little extra, it gives both you and the owner more security; on your end if the deal goes sour you can do a chargeback either through PayPal or through your credit card (always fund your PayPal payments with a credit card, NOT through your bank account!). It also keeps the owner from having to worry about bad checks or phony money orders. The usual deal is that ½ of the payment is required up front, with the other half paid once you receive your reservation papers from DVC with your name on them. Once you're paid up the DVC owner will be able to book the Dining Plan for you (I advise against it, as I'll discuss later) and will also be able to enter your flight reservations into the Disney Magical Express system.

Unfortunately, in this world you always have to be prepared for a scam, and renting points is no different. Since Disney does not officially condone point rentals, they're not going to be able to do anything for you if you get scammed. While I have only heard of one horror story (which was eventually resolved) and while most DVC owners are honest hard-working people just like you and me, you do still need to be careful and protect yourself. Here are some tips on how to do that:

- Draw up a contract and have both parties sign it. There are many available on Disboards, although most owners have a standard contract they always use. A contract gives peace of mind to both parties, mainly because it puts into writing the expectations of both the owner and renter, so that there is no confusion about details later on, after payment has already been made. Also, in a worst case scenario, a contract should come in handy in small claims court.

❤ Check references. Anyone renting DVC points should have a list of people they've rented to before who are willing to vouch for them. Be sure to contact these references to verify that they were satisfied with their rental transaction. If the owner has never rented before, at the very least make sure they have a decent post count on the board you contacted them on. If they don't, I'd be wary that they're a fly-by-night scammer. Stay clear and find another owner.

❤ As mentioned before, pay via PayPal using your credit card so you can do a chargeback if necessary.

❤ Once you find a trustworthy owner, stick with them! If you have a good renting experience, you should always contact that owner about upcoming vacations to see if they have points or reservations available.

If you're still feeling a bit queasy about renting points, there is an alternate way to do it. You can use a 3rd party service, such as David's Vacation Club Rentals, at www.dvcrequest.com/ . David acts as the middleman between you and the owner, and thus you're paying him, not the owner. It's almost like an escrow account. David deals with all of the contracts, and has a bank of owners he works with who he knows are trustworthy. However, you definitely pay for this added layer of security: David charges $13/point, which is a premium of $3-$4 over what you'd normally pay. It's still quite a bargain, but to be honest, if you take the precautions listed above, I just don't think it's necessary.

PARK TICKETS

Sneaking In:

It's a warm August morning in 1995 at EPCOT. Three of us, all college age nerds, stand in front of the ticket kiosks, marveling at the ticket prices, which had been significantly cheaper just weeks before.

"Fuck this," says Newmeyer, a longtime friend and fellow Disney addict. "I can't afford this shit anymore!" He's wearing a black trenchcoat, a black fedora, and a patchy beard; not exactly inconspicuous in the middle of the summer, even in these pre-Columbine days.

McGeorge, a wiry MacGyver look-alike, stares at Newmeyer. "What can you do?" he asks. "If we want in, we gotta buy a ticket!"

"I'm jumping the gate!" Newmeyer proclaims, loud enough for everyone in the near vicinity to hear. And he proceeds to stand at the gate on the far right side of the entrance (where the laundry carts used to come in and out) for a good half hour, getting up the nerve. McGeorge and I watch, knowing that this is more exciting than Spaceship Earth, at least for the moment.

Finally, Newmeyer calmly opens the gate and saunters into the park. He turns around and gives us the thumbs up. McGeorge and I look at each other with a "What the fuck? Why have we been paying for tickets?" look.

Ten seconds later two security officers wearing Hawaiian shirts walk up alongside Newmeyer and casually take his arms, leading him backstage. He looks back at us in panic before he disappears behind a façade of manicured plants. This being pre-cellphone days we simply wait outside the park entrance, passing the time by telling confused tourists that "the entire park is inside the big golf ball."

Hours later, Newmeyer reappears, disheveled and wiping away tears. "I'm banned from the parks for life," he sobs. "I can't ever go back! They took my picture, they took my fucking fingerprints, they made a copy of my driver's license, they took my social security number.... They'll send me straight to jail if I come anywhere near here again!"

"Ah, that's bullshit," we say, patting him on the shoulder. "Out of all of the people who come here every day, how are they going to keep you out?"

Newmeyer is consoled, and we go back to our off-site hotel, get drunk, and try unsuccessfully to score chicks. The next day we buy tickets for Disney/MGM Studios and Newmeyer gets in with no problems. He promptly forgets about the whole "banned for life" thing.

Four years pass, and Newmeyer calls Disney Reservations to book his honeymoon, asking for a room at the Caribbean Beach Resort for him and his soon to be wife. "Hold for a minute", the cast member says after he gives his address and credit card number.

Minutes pass. Newmeyer gets a weird nagging feeling in the pit of his stomach. "Something's going on here..." he thinks as he nervously chews the end of the pen he's holding.

A different person comes on the line. "Sir, we're trying to verify your credit card information. Did you used to live on xxxx," asks this stern new voice, reciting Newmeyer's address from four years ago.

"Yeah, sure," says Newmeyer, slowly. He jolts as that nagging feeling in the pit of his stomach suddenly turns into a full blown memory. "Oh, shit, you have got to be kidding me...." he whispers, feeling sick.

"Sir," says the voice on the line, "I must inform you that you are not welcome on Walt Disney World property. If we find that you are on the property during these dates, you will be arrested for trespassing." The connection drops abruptly, and Newmeyer is left to tell his fiancé how her dreams of a Disney honeymoon are shattered.

As my dumbass friend Newmeyer clearly illustrated, unless you want to risk being banned for life and arrested, you need a ticket if you want to get into the parks. Let it be known that this book does not endorse sneaking into the parks! However, if you still insist on sneaking in, here are some tips:

- The aforementioned trio of Newmeyer, McGeorge and I spent an inordinate amount of time trying to find "back entrances" to the WDW parks. We actually trod through a swamp at one point, thinking that it would lead to an unguarded area of one of the parks, when actuality we came right up against a razor wire topped fence. The only legitimate back entrances are there for employees, and those are heavily guarded by multiple security gates. So scour Google Maps all you want, but trust me when I say that the perimeters of the parks are secured.

- Years ago you used to be able to stand outside the exit gates and ask paying guests for their ticket stubs as they left the parks (or you'd just dig in the trash for them). You could then go to the entry gates to gain "re-entry", and when the attendant unsuccessfully checked your fluorescent handstamp under the blacklight you'd have to try to convince them that you must have washed it off. Now, with the new biometric finger scanning system, they don't fall for this shit anymore. Finger doesn't match, no handstamp, no fucking way you're getting in. We actually went so far as to "borrow" a handstamp from behind an unmanned gate at one point, but again, it's unlikely this trick is going to work now that the finger scanners provide a second layer of bullshit detection.

- All of the parks now have security people checking bags at entrances. If you try to sneak past security you will be immediately arrested. Go through like everyone else, and try not to look suspicious (i.e., don't wear a black trench coat and a fedora). Don't try to carry in any weapons or alcohol.
- Once you get past security, the gates at the parks stretch for quite a distance, usually with the entrances in the middle, and exit gates on the far left and right. Thus, for gate jumping you have two options:

  1. Sneak in through the exits.

  Depending on the time of day there could be anywhere from 1-5 exit gates open. Obviously you'll want to go later in the evening when there are fewer employees per gate, and more people are leaving so you can get lost in the crowd. You'll want to go through the handicapped entrance as opposed to jumping the turnstile.

  Honestly the only time jumping the exit gates is going to be even slightly non-risky is right after Illuminations/Fantasmic/Wishes ends, and the parks are clearing out. But at that point, why are you even bothering? In fact, a CM tells me that anytime after the evening entertainment finishes is essentially "open gate time" because they need all available manpower to herd people out of the park. So if you really just want to visit the park for 30-45 minutes, nobody is going to try to stop you from walking in at the end of the night.

Magic Kingdom Exit Queue

As an aside, there is no good time to jump the exit gates at Animal Kingdom because it closes too early, and there is no big event at the end of the evening to cause massive exit crowds.

2. Sneak in through the entrances.

"I don't like hearing about people jumping the turnstiles," a CM told me. "Too many times I've seen kids jump the turnstiles and they end up kicking the gate attendants in the process, sometimes on purpose. A lot of the attendants are older folks, and I've seen them get seriously hurt. It ends up looking like a scene from "Clockwork Orange", with these sad old people lying on the ground bleeding, and a bunch of hooligan kids running off laughing. I don't care as much that these kids are getting in for free, because they probably wouldn't have paid regardless, but when they start hurting other Cast Members, that's when I get mad." Moral of the story: don't jump the turnstiles – use the handicapped gates instead! Oh, and don't kick old people. Unless they deserve it.

Unfortunately for Disney's bottom line, this method of sneaking in seems fairly foolproof. Especially in the mornings during holidays there is simply no way you can be stopped if you decide to walk through a handicapped entry gate. The gate attendant will yell at you to stop, but assuming you've worn non-descript clothes you will blend into the crowd in a millisecond.

I've personally seen this method used many times, and the best part is it's usually done by foreign tourists who have no intention of sneaking in, they're just oblivious to their surroundings and think they're bypassing the first of many long lines!

Honestly, sneaking into the parks is just plain stupid unless you're only there for a day and don't care if you get kicked out. Because do you really want to spend every day of your vacation worrying if that'll be the day you go to Disney Jail? Wouldn't you rather just pay for tickets (a relatively small amount compared to the rest of your vacation expenses) for some peace of mind?

Then again… go ahead and do it! Sneak in, get caught, and take pictures of Disney Jail for me so that I can exploit the fruits of your misfortune in the next edition of this book!

That said, there are ways you can get free tickets to WDW, which is

Epcot's Entrance queue - the far right is the service entrance

Disney Hollywood Studios Entry Gate

almost the same as sneaking in, except it's (mostly) legit. You have two options for free tickets: 1) timeshare presentations, and 2) becoming good friends with a 15-Year+ cast member.

Don't kick old people!

Free Tickets from Timeshare Presentations:

Do you have nerves of steel and the willpower of an annoying mule who won't move no matter how much you yell at him? Do you not mind wasting hours of your precious vacation touring a resort that can't hold a candle to any of the WDW Deluxes and listening to a greasy salesman who is going to berate and insult you? Do you really, really, really not want to pay for your tickets? Well then, you might be a perfect candidate for a Timeshare Presentation!

Drive down International Boulevard and you'll see plenty of booths advertising these things. Or just go to the lobby of one of the multitude of cheap off-site motels and they'll likely have a kiosk promoting "FREE DISNEY TICKETS!!!" Tell the person at the booth or kiosk that you're interested in attending the timeshare presentation, and they'll tell you when and where to go. Make sure you get the details up front! Usually you AND your spouse need to attend, and in return for 90 minutes of your time you'll get two free tickets to a WDW park. If these conditions are not specified in writing, move onto the next booth.

But getting into one of these presentations is the easy part. Getting out is the chore. My wife and I discovered this unpleasant dichotomy when we went on a timeshare presentation pretty soon after we were married. We didn't have a lot of spending money, so free tickets seemed like a great way to have some extra cash for a romantic dinner at La Cellier. Wrong!

We scheduled a presentation with a company who'd sent us a mailer months earlier and they told us they'd pick us up at our Disney resort, so we didn't even need to rent a car. Since we'd used DME, renting a car to get free tickets wouldn't have made much financial sense. But we learned the first lesson of timeshare presentations: Never, EVER get into a car with your salesman!

Anyway, the sales guy drives up in a nice BMW, and he's got this charming Greek accent and is wearing a white suit and looks like George Hamilton, except not quite as leathery. So there goes my wife, right? She's fawning all over him, and I have to admit the guy is pretty suave. We get in the car and he actually seems nice and he shows us pictures of his family and then tells us how he was a double-agent spy for the UK in Greece, which doesn't make much sense, but why would someone lie about that? And then I realize I've been sucked in by this guy and we've already driven 35 minutes and I have no idea where we are! Like, we're in the middle of a swamp somewhere!

I'm a little freaked now, but I try my best to calmly ask George Hamilton where the fuck we are, and he says, "Oh, we're almost to the resort," but it comes out sounding more like, "Oh, we're driving out to a secluded location where I can rape you and your wife and then feed you to the alligators!" I look at my wife with an "oh shit!" expression and she's still looking at George with googly eyes but then she sees my expression of horror and suddenly snaps out of it, looks out the window at our desolate surroundings, and then she starts freaking out a bit, too.

Just as I'm about to fucking karate chop George in the throat and steal his car, we actually do pull up to a "resort". The first thing we see is this really nice St.Augustine sort of old-Spanish building with a bunch of balconies overlooking a big lake with a boat dock. It's pretty impressive. Except then it becomes plainly obvious that there's this one nice building in the center and then a bunch of dilapidated husks of identical buildings around the rest of the lake, all abandoned and overgrown and looking like they're covered with mildew or something. It's creepy.

George walks us into the main building and into a big conference room, where there are a few other couples who have obviously been here a while. He offers us some sodas and cookies, and tells us that now we're going to "get down to business". So he goes through this whole spiel that sounds like an awesome deal, and I'm almost convinced, but then I remember that a) we have no money, and b) this place is in the middle of nowhere and most of the buildings are in ruins, and there's no fucking way I'd ever want to vacation here. Which I pretty much tell George, in so many words.

Well, he's not fazed a bit. He cuts the price by 50% and starts going on about how we can trade into other resorts all around the world, blah blah blah. We hear a champagne cork pop a few tables over as a beaten-down couple celebrates their new major investment. George looks agitated, and it goes downhill from there. Long story short he keeps talking, I keep saying "no", he drops the price like eight more times, I still say, "no", and he gets increasingly angry and starts going on about how he has to feed his kids, and how I'm making them starve or some such nonsense.

That's when I look at my watch and notice three hours have gone by since we left our resort. Now I'm pissed. I tell George flat out that we're not buying a timeshare at this dump, and that if I wanted to buy a timeshare to begin with I'd do it on eBay where I can literally get it for a penny, and that we just want our Disney tickets and want to go back to our resort.

Now he's really fuming but I can tell he doesn't want to freak out in front of the other couples, so he says "Fine, come with me to get your tickets," and brings us into a small office where another guy is sitting behind a desk.

This office looks like it's from the 50s with dirty wood paneling and a rusted metal desk, and the guy behind the desk has a bad toupee that also looks like it's from the 50s. My wife and I sit in equally rusty chairs as George looms behind us, arms crossed. So then toupee guy proceeds to basically yell at us for ten minutes about how we're shitty people because we've wasted George's time and now he might get fired and he's yelling at me about how I'm a cheapskate, and it's really pretty awful and my wife is crying but I don't want to hit the guy because I want to get out of there with our Disney tickets and if I knock him out we probably won't get them! So I just sit there and smile and finally he stops yelling and I calmly say, "I want my goddamned tickets, and I want to go back to our resort now or I'm calling the police and telling them you kidnapped us."

Well, this shuts toupee guy up, and he slams down two vouchers (not even tickets) on the metal table and rust flies up everywhere. "Here's your goddamned tickets you motherfuckers!" he's yelling, beet red. "But we're not driving you back! Read the contract, it says nothing about return transportation! Hahaha! Now get the hell out of my face!" he screams as his toupee flops around, and he points to a door. Him and George are laughing and calling us "motherfuckers" as we walk out of the door, which leads to a rickety fire escape ladder which ends next to a dumpster with what looks like a swamp around it.

So we finally get down there and our shoes and socks are ruined from the swamp mud and I end up calling our resort back at Disney because I have no idea where we are and I'm not sure what else to do. Luckily they know exactly where we are, obviously having received this same phone call many times, and call a cab for us. The cab ends up costing over $120, which is almost as much as the fucking tickets cost (more if you count our ruined shoes). We end up getting back to our resort almost 6 hours after we'd left, so we basically wasted a whole day of our vacation. Plus, we missed our La Cellier reservations. FAIL!

My wife and I laugh about it now, but at the time it wasn't funny and nearly ruined our vacation. Totally not worth it. Although, from what I've been told the DVC tours are quite nice, the sales people are ultra-low pressure, and you even get ice cream and Fast Passes. But they still get pissed if you tell them you're going to buy resale instead.

Befriending a 15-Year+ Cast Member:

First of all, just finding someone who has worked at WDW for fifteen years is nothing short of a miracle. The pay is shit, the working conditions are restrictive, and frankly they don't treat their staff very well. But some people just love Disney, and are willing to overlook all of the crap to maintain their dream of working for The Mouse.

Anyway, if you're lucky enough to find a "lifer", you should immediately become good friends with that person. Because they are in possession of the coveted "Silver" Main Entrance Pass, which allows them to bring three people a day into the parks for free (some blackout dates do apply)!

An authentic Silver Main Entrance Pass

To be fair, full-time CMs who have worked there for more than 3 months but less than 15 years get "Blue" Main Gate passes, which allow entry for three people 16 times during the year. But my experience is that these CMs are really stingy with their 16 entries, usually because they think that despite their poor financial status and crappy, irregular working hours, they'll still somehow find a non-staff boyfriend/girlfriend to take to the parks. Think again, losers!

And that's why I don't have any friends who are CMs.

Reseller Scams:

Okay, so you've decided you don't want to jump the gates and go to Disney Jail, and you don't want to waste a day doing a timeshare presentation and possibly getting stranded in a swamp. You also either live nowhere near the parks or you're a big loser and/or an insensitive and cruel person like me, and thus you have no CM friends to get you into the parks for free. So you've given up, and are ready to hand over your wallet to

Disney so it can make sweet love to your cash and leave some tickets on the nightstand when it's done. Not so fast! Why are you giving up so easily? Why are you so eager to prostitute out your hard-earned cash?!

It turns out that there actually are reputable ticket resellers who will sell you WDW tickets for moderately cheaper than the standard gate prices! My authorized reseller recommendation is Undercover Tourist (http://www.undercovertourist.com). I've used them multiple times and have always received friendly service and the correct tickets, which show up in an unmarked envelope and come wrapped in plastic. These are actual WDW tickets, not the vouchers you'd get at a timeshare presentation, and they work perfectly.

As of this writing, the standard Undercover Tourist discount on a 6-day Adult Park Hopper is $16, which isn't bad, especially if you have a large family. However, you can get an even bigger discount ($22) from them if you sign up for the MouseSavers newsletter at http://www.mousesavers.com/newsletter.html . This monthly newsletter is a great compendium of current discounts/closures/news for both WDW and Disneyland, but more importantly, it contains a secret "newsletter only" link to Undercover Tourist that will give you bigger discounts!

As an aside, another cool thing about Undercover Tourist is that they offer the UK/Ireland-only 14 or 21 day "Ultimate Ticket". If you're going to be at WDW for two or three weeks (you lucky bastard!) this might be the way to go. The 14-day Ultimate Ticket gives you two weeks of park hopping, plus Water Park, DisneyQuest, and Wide World of Sports access. Right now after converting pounds to dollars the adult 14-day Ultimate is going for $373, which is actually $2 cheaper than the 10-day Park Hopper + Water Park ticket! So you're getting 7 more days for $2 less. What a bargain!

However, you might be thinking that these are pretty tepid discounts, and I can't argue that they only amount to a pair of mouse ears for each member of your family, or a few harf-and-harfs at the Rose and Crown. If you're like me, you're still looking for even bigger discounts, and have drooled at the signs all around the Kissimmee/Orlando advertising ultra-cheap tickets. These resellers pawn their wares in booths, gas stations, and even in reputable hotels. And lo and behold, if you go into one of these places they actually are selling tickets for dirt cheap. We're talking up to 50% off the gate price! Now, that's a discount!

One of the many ticket reseller booths in Orlando

But as the old saying goes, if it seems too good to be true, it probably is. After doing extensive research on these resellers, I've found that literally 100% of them are illegal scams, and if you buy tickets from them you will likely not be able to use those tickets to gain entry to the parks.

Here's how the scam works: a departing vacationer is offered a decent amount of cash ($20-$50) to sell any ticket with unused days on it to one of these illegal reseller operations. Maybe the tourist accidentally bought too many days and can't use them all, or maybe their vacation got cut short; the reasoning behind the confused mind of a tourist is unimportant to the scammers. So now the reseller has a ticket with (for example) two days left on it, and those two days expire in 10 days (Magic Your Way passes are good for 14 days after first being run through a turnstile). The scam reseller can turn around and sell this as a two-day ticket to unsuspecting tourists looking for a big discount over gate prices. Furthermore, they actively encourage people to add days to the used Magic Your Way ticket (which can be done at greatly reduced rates, as low as $5/day) so that they can come back to the booth at the end of their vacation and sell back any unused days for an even bigger overall discount. Brilliant!

There are four big problems with this, from the perspective of someone looking to purchase a used ticket:

1. It's illegal. It specifically says on the tickets that they can't be resold. In fact, it's a felony. However, it's not necessarily illegal to buy used tickets, just to resell them, so from the tourist's point of view, it's a legal gray area.
2. There's a signature on the back of the ticket. No biggie, the resellers usually get these off prior to selling them by applying a special acid to the signature strip, although observant CMs can spot this a mile away.
3. All of the parks in WDW use biometric finger scanning. This measures the length of your fingers from knuckle to knuckle. If your finger isn't the same size as the one already recorded on the ticket, chances are you're not getting through the gate.
4. This is the real kicker: There's no way of verifying how many days are on the ticket until you're actually on Disney property. So you might get there and find that there aren't any days left on the ticket, and you got totally scammed.

It used to be that if you bought a phony or used ticket that didn't work you could go to Guest Services and they'd be really understanding and nice about it and give you a new one, but now they're wise to the whole underground reseller racket and are completely unsympathetic to the plight of scammed tourists. How do I know this? Because I took one for the team and bought such a ticket. The buying part was easy: I went into a gas station, made sure there weren't any cops around, and paid cash for a Two-Day MYW base ticket. Using the ticket at the parks was where the whole thing fell apart. Here's how it went down:

The crowds are light as I approach the turnstile at The Magic Kingdom, put my used ticket through the slot, and place my finger on the scanner. It doesn't work. The CM tells me to do it again, with the other hand. Still doesn't work.

Me: "Huh, that's weird."

CM: "Are you sure this is your ticket?"

Me: "Uhhh….."

CM: "Sir, you'll need to go to Guest Services to get this resolved. Have a magical day!"

Me: "Okay. Thanks"

So I go to Guest Services and hand over my ticket.

Me: "It doesn't work when I put my finger on the thingy."

CM: "Did you use the same finger you used the first time you went through the gate with this ticket?"

Me: "Not exactly."

CM: "Sir, where did you purchase this ticket?"

Me: "From a gas station."

CM: "We're sorry, but we're not able to accept tickets purchased from unauthorized resellers. Unfortunately you'll need to buy a new ticket. I can help you with that now, if you'd like."

Me: "So I just lost a bunch of money, right? And there's nothing you can do about it?"

CM: "That is our policy, sir."

Me: "Bummer. Can I get my ticket back, so I can at least sell it back to the gas station?"

CM: "Unfortunately since it was resold illegally I will need to confiscate it. However, here is a collectible "What Will You Celebrate" pin. Have a magical day!"

The CM gives me a little pin and I smile weakly and walk away. I lost money so you don't have to!

However, I've been in line during busy times of the day, and a lot of times if the finger scanner doesn't work the CM will punch in some code at the turnstile and just let the guest through. I gather the scanners aren't wholly reliable, and most CMs don't care enough about resold tickets to hold up the line and incur the wrath of impatient guests. But this is the exception rather than the rule.

If you're a real sleazeball, there is one surefire way to get around the biometric scanner: act like you're disabled. Borrow a wheelchair and have a friend push you to the gate and say that you can't lift your arms up to the scanner. The CM will run the used ticket for you and let you through the handicapped gate, no questions asked. But that's some super-bad karma to pull down just for discounted theme park tickets!

Another way to save money on tickets, if you don't mind possibly going to jail at the end of your vacation (real jail, not Disney Jail – big difference), is by taking advantage of the other side of the resale scam: sell your unused days. The easiest (and cheapest) way to do this is to buy more days than you know you'll use from Undercover Tourist. That way you're not only getting a discount for the days you will use, but your unused days are also discounted, which means you have a larger profit margin when you go to sell those unused days. And the more days you buy, the cheaper they are, to the point where after the 4th day each additional day averages out to about $5.

So say you intend to stay 7 days at WDW (a regular 7-day MYW costs $263 at the gate). You'd buy a 10-day MYW base ticket from Undercover Tourist for $266, only $3 more than Disney's gate price for a 7-day. At the end of your vacation you drive over to one of the reseller places on your way home and sell your remaining 3 days for $50. Now your 7-day MYW ticket has ended up costing you only $216, which is a $47 discount from the gate prices! There are also ways you can work out even bigger discounts by purchasing and reselling the various water park, park hopper, and non-expiration options, although the combinations of Undercover Tourist prices vs. reseller buyback prices are so numerous that finding the sweet spot of maximum profit might take a fair amount of calculator action.

As an addendum, I did talk to a detective completely off the record about these reseller scams. The detective told me that yes, the Orange County Sheriff's Office is aggressively going after the employees who operate the reseller booths and kiosks because it is believed that most of these operations link back to a bigger crime ring, which they're anxious to bust up. However, at this point (as in, this might change at any time) the detective says they are absolutely not arresting tourists caught buying or selling tickets to the resellers, because the majority of the tourists have no idea that they're a part of any legal wrongdoings. In other words, if you get caught, this is one of those rare cases where playing dumb might actually keep you out of jail.

FREE PARKING

If you've decided to stay offsite and rent a car (dumb!) or are a local driving in for a day trip, you'll likely be shocked at the cost of parking. $14 to park isn't necessarily outrageous by Manhattan standards, but when you consider you're paying $14 for the privilege of spending hundreds more for tickets, food, and merchandise, you realize that it's just another cash grab. They know you'll pay the $14 because it's a relatively small amount in comparison to what you'll be spending throughout your trip, and if you're willing to shell out all of that cash you're certainly not going to turn around and go home because of an overpriced parking fee. It's the first of many times during the day that Disney bends you over and gives you the shaft.

But you don't have to take it! There are ways to get free parking at WDW!

At the Resorts:

It used to be that you could pull up to the far right gate at Magic Kingdom, tell them you were visiting a friend at The Contemporary, and they'd let you through without paying, no questions asked. Same thing with The Boardwalk as free parking for Epcot. But I guess eventually Disney caught onto this trick and they stopped letting people through the gates unless they had a valid, verifiable dining reservation. However, this is fairly easy to deal with as long as you plan in advance. A few days before your trip call Disney Reservations and make reservation at one of the restaurants in the hotel where you want to park. They'll put you on a daily list, and the person at the gate will check that list and let you through. During peak seasons they'll give you a 3-hour parking pass, but I've found that if you "accidentally forget" to put the pass on your dashboard you'll be able to park in a resort lot all day without being towed.

Here are some resort/restaurant suggestions for each park:

- ❤ Magic Kingdom: O'Hana at The Polynesian. Park and either walk over to The Magic Kingdom or take the monorail two stops over. Or if you're really feeling adventurous and don't feel like worrying about the 3-hour limitation, you can pretend like you're driving to the Polynesian lot but instead continue past the resort (at this point you're out of sight of the main gate attendants) and circle back around to the regular Magic Kingdom lot, effectively bypassing the main gate parking fee.
- ❤ Epcot/DHS: Flying Fish Café at The Boardwalk. The Boardwalk has the biggest lot (including an overflow lot across the street) and from the lobby it's a 5 minute walk to the International Gateway at Epcot, or a 15 minute walk to DHS. You can also take one of the complimentary boats to either location. FYI, They WILL enforce the 3-hour limit during The Food and Wine Festival at Epcot.

Go right at the Main Gate and circle past The Polynesian for free parking

- Animal Kingdom: Nope, nada, nothing. There are no resorts within walking distance to Animal Kingdom. However, if you're lucky you might be able to make a reservation at The Rainforest Café and either get free parking or get your parking validated inside the restaurant.

- If all else fails you can always park for free at Downtown Disney. However, there are NO busses from Downtown Disney to any of the parks. So you'll have to take a boat or bus to a resort, and then take a bus, boat, or monorail from that resort to the park you want to visit. Of course, after all of this transferring you'll probably have wasted an hour of your precious vacation time, so it's up to you to decide if that hour is worth less than the $14 it would have cost you to pay for parking.

AAA Diamond Pass:

This isn't free parking, but can be used in conjunction with the above tips. If you book your vacation through AAA you will receive a parking pass that allows you access to the Diamond Lot at each park. The Diamond Lot is usually right up front near the entrance so you don't have to fight your way onto the tram, you can just walk to the entrance. If you've ever waited for a WDW parking tram you know that they can be extremely crowded, and with all of the stops it can take you 30 minutes or more to get to the actual gate.

Although they don't advertise this fact, you actually only need to purchase your Park Hoppers through AAA to get the Diamond Pass, not your entire vacation. AAA offers a decent discount on Park Hoppers, although not as much as Undercover Tourist, so it's up to you to figure out if it's worth the extra expense of booking through AAA to get this convenience.

However, eBay again comes to the rescue. You can buy a AAA parking pass on eBay for less than $30, which is good for the length of your stay. If you're renting a car, staying a week, renting a DVC, and purchasing your tickets via Undercover Tourist (or have Annual Passes) this is probably a great deal for the convenience it offers.

EATING/DRINKING THERE

There's no such thing as cheap food or booze for sale in WDW. Sure, there might be bargains that bring the costs down a bit, but compared to your local grocery store, corner bar, or chain restaurant, all consumables in WDW are way overpriced.

On their end, the reasoning for these high prices is "You're stuck here, suckers, so deal with it!" They know the chances of you leaving the WDW Resort for a meal are extremely small (especially if you've used DME and couldn't drive off-property if you wanted to) so they jack up prices to crazy levels. And unfortunately, with the advent of the Dining Plan and "Free Dining", prices have continued to go up over the years as quality and portion sizes have decreased.

If you went to a restaurant at home with such high prices and mediocre food, you'd likely complain to the manager and would never go back there again. So why put up with it at WDW? "Oh, we're on vacation, we can splurge a little," is the typical response. Well, sure, that makes sense if you're splurging on high quality food with excellent service, but it seems like the days where management saw the restaurants at WDW as a source of pride instead of a cash cow are mostly gone. There are a few exceptions – a certain entrée at a certain sit-down that is world-class, or a certain appetizer at a counter service that's a hell of a bargain, but those exceptions are quickly disappearing.

So stop throwing your hard earned money away! I can't tell you how to make the food any better at WDW, but at the very least I can tell you how to come away from your vacation with a full stomach and a lot more cash in your pockets.

"Free Dining" is Not Free!!!:

If you really think that Disney is going to give you something for free, I have a bridge in Brooklyn I'd like to sell you. Their "Free Dining" promotion gets everyone up in a tizzy, because they hear the word "free" and start freaking out. But there's nothing "free" about it. You're actually paying out the ass for it!

The way the deal works is that you buy a package that includes your room, tickets, and the Disney Dining Plan, aka DDP (Quick Service if you're staying at a Value Resort, or the regular plan if you're at a Moderate), except the DDP is supposedly "free". So they give you a single price for your entire vacation, and aside from souvenirs, once you hit the ground everything is already paid for.

The problems with this are numerous:

1. You're not allowed to use any other discounts on top of this "free dining" promotion. So the "buy 4 get 3 free" deal, where you get 7 days at a resort for the price of 4? Nope, can't do it. $500 gift card if you reserve a 7 day vacation? Nope. 40% off code? Not a chance. You have to pay full rack rates for your rooms, and no discounts on your tickets, either, which means Undercover Tourist is out the window. And to be perfectly frank, only suckers pay rack rate at WDW.

    It used to be that you could probably do just as well at "Free Dining" as you could with these other discounts IF you were staying in a Value Resort, because everyone got the same version of the DDP, regardless of what kind of resort you stayed at. But now that they've changed the "Free Dining" for Values to "Quick Service" restaurants only, that slight edge is put into the negative. In other words, YOU ARE LOSING MONEY BY GETTING "FREE DINING" INSTEAD OF USING THE OTHER DISCOUNTS OUT THERE!!!

2. The DDP itself is overpriced. Just a few years ago, when it first started, it was a good deal. Each day you'd get a quick service meal, 2 snacks, and a table service meal with an appetizer, entrée, drink, and desert (the tip was also included) for $35/day. You still had to eat a buttload of food each day to come out ahead, but at least you COULD come out ahead and have it be a decent bargain. But now you don't get the appetizer, you only get one snack, and the tip isn't included. That's a reduction of 30% at least, and at the price has increased to $48/day. As only Disney can, they've increased the price and decreased the service, and people are still buying it. What a rip-off.

   Do me a favor: visit http://allears.net/din/dining.htm, check the prices on the restaurants you want to eat at, and then add up what you'll spend per person per day (without gorging yourself). Most likely over the course of 7 days that amount is going to be equal to or less than what you would pay for the Dining Plan.

3. If you're on the DDP, by the end of your vacation you're going to be so fucking sick of Disney food that you won't ever want to eat again. But since you already paid for it you'll feel obligated to keep those dining reservations and keep gorging yourself until it becomes an unpleasant burden. Why would you want to do that to yourself on vacation? Wouldn't you rather just eat what you want, when you want, knowing that it's okay if you want to skip a dinner ADR because you ate too much at lunch and you're not hungry?

4. "But I like that it's prepaid and I can budget for it," you say. Yes, budgeting is important, and not being able to go over budget is a nice feature of the DDP. But you could also stash away the same amount of cash on a Disney Gift Card, and only use that to pay for your meals. Every time you use it the receipt printout tells you how much is left on your card, which is a great way to manage your

spending.

5. WDW's food quality and portion sizes have gone downhill big time since the DDP came around. Since the number crunchers have to make a profit on DDP, they can't have any of the food at any of the restaurants be too different in price or quality. The reason being that if word gets around that there's one spectacular restaurant, or one amazingly great (but expensive) thing on a certain menu, then everyone on the DDP will go to that one restaurant or order that one most expensive item on the menu, and Disney will lose money (in fact this has happened – as of this writing La Cellier, which often receives great reviews for their food and service, has gone from 1 Table Service credit to 2, effectively doubling the price of the meal. They also got rid of the really high-quality steaks there years ago). As a result, none of the restaurants stand out anymore, and all of the food is kinda blah.

Cheap/Free Dining for Drunks and Foodies:

So what's the alternative to "free dining" and the DDP if you took DME and can't drive to cheaper off-site restaurants? On the surface, it seems like your options are to either starve, which isn't a pleasant way to spend your vacation, or pay out of pocket, which can get prohibitively expensive if you're doing it for every meal considering the prices Disney charges even at the Quick Service restaurants. And what if you want to get totally shit-faced drunk? As someone with a fairly high tolerance, the prospect of buying enough booze at WDW to get good and blotto is enough to sober me back up immediately. Last time I was there a regular 12oz bottle of Bud was $6 at the resort's General Store!

Well, there are options! You CAN eat and drink at WDW on a budget!

♥ Split an entrée and an appetizer. Many of the portions are too big anyway, especially at the Counter Service restaurants, so why not order a single appetizer and entrée for two people and split it? Of course, you can't do this on the DDP because each person has to order their own separate entrée, but if you're not on the DDP you'll find that this is usually just the right amount of food for two people.

♥ Or you can order more food and bring back leftovers! This works especially well if you're eating at Epcot and are staying at one of the

Epcot Resorts, because you can walk back after your meal, put the leftovers in the fridge, and go right back to the park. I end up doing this a lot and leftovers make a great breakfast or late-night snack.

❤ Don't eat breakfast, then go to a buffet for lunch, stay there and eat for at least two hours, and then don't eat dinner either. WDW buffets don't end up costing much more per person than a full table service meal, but you can eat a lot more, especially if you stick around for a while and let the first round of gluttony settle. I personally recommend Boma or Tusker House, although Germany gets an honorable mention for the surprisingly reasonably priced liters of beer and awesome entertainment.

Tip: The dining rooms at these buffets are usually so sprawling and packed that it becomes very easy to secretly load up a plate of muffins, rolls, brownies, or whatever, and dump them into a large freezer bag, which can then be stashed in a purse or backpack. I used to wrap up cookies in a napkin and put them in my jacket pocket. Yeah, it's pretty ghetto, but you'll forget all about that when you're eating Zebra Domes in your resort Jacuzzi later that night.

❤ Taking this one step further is a tip that might actually be illegal, is definitely immoral, but is also totally fucking delicious! Pecos Bill's and Cosmic Ray's at The Magic Kingdom have epic toppings bars. Lettuce, tomatoes, salsa, shredded cheese, cheese sauce, sautéed mushrooms and onions, lettuce, and a variety of other condiments make this a vegetarian's dream buffet. Bring a few paper plates from your resort, head over to one of these two counter service restaurants, and load up on free toppings! I've seen people bring their own tortilla chips and make a monster taco salad, or they bring their own rolls and make a great grilled veggie sandwich. Again, I think this is technically theft, but there are no signs saying "toppings bar for paying customers only", so I figure it's fair game.

❤ As long as we're talking about theft, you can get all the free food you could ever want in The Utilidors or behind the scenes at Epcot. For whatever reason they leave racks and racks of food sitting around out in the open. Mostly I saw sodas and rolls, but I'm sure if you looked around you could find more. Not that I'm advocating theft; this is more like a desert island scenario, like maybe The Mad Hatter stole your wallet and ran down to The Utilidors and you followed him and got lost and couldn't find your way out and instead of resorting to cannibalism while waiting to be rescued you ate stolen bread.

The Entrance to Peco Bill's, home of the Topping Bar

I recently heard of an actual food theft: A large table at California Grill ordered all of the most expensive stuff off the menu, including many bottles of wine. One of the big draws of the California Grill is the amazing view of the fireworks at The Magic Kingdom, but not every table is situated alongside a window. So usually when the fireworks start going off, a bunch of people who are sitting in the middle of the restaurant go out to the deck (right above my secret sex location) to watch the show. Well, this large group of big eaters and drinkers filed out to the deck with everyone else but instead of watching the fireworks they went down the steps to the 14th floor and presumably took the elevator to the first floor and drove off! I

Free sauteed mushrooms and cheese sauce

Free tomatoes, lettuce, and shredded cheese

feel bad for the poor waiter who had to explain that to his manager, and assume that if this keeps happening they will eventually put in safeguards to prevent it.

There are also a few methods of getting free desserts by outright lying. For example, when you check into your resort tell them it's your anniversary or birthday or bah mitzvah or some other sort of celebration (be sure if you say it's your anniversary that you and your significant other get your story straight, because you'll have about a thousand CMs congratulating you and asking how many years it's been). You'll be given a button to wear that says what you're celebrating. You must wear this at all times! At almost every table service restaurant you'll get a free dessert to celebrate whatever occasion you lied about! We got an incredible gelato at Il Mulino, a sundae at Sci-Fi Dine In, chocolate cake at both Coral Reef and Brown Derby, and champagne at California Grill. By wearing this button you might also get other perks such as Fastpasses, room upgrades, comp'd drinks at bars, etc.

Dan, an acquaintance of mine (i.e., not someone I'd be proud to call a friend) routinely pulls another scam almost every time he dines at WDW. He's a fairly distinguished-looking guy, mid-40s with graying temples, and always wearing a sports coat. But inside lurks the biggest cheapskate I've ever met.

"Okay, Dan, explain the scam," I say, pronouncing his name the same way I'd say "disgusting piece of shit".

"It's pretty simple, although it only works once at any particular restaurant" says Dan, his eyes twinkling with glee. "Luckily there are almost two hundred restaurants in Walt Disney World, and I'm not even a quarter of the way through them yet!

"Everyone knows there's a huge bug problem in Florida, especially with roaches and ants. So before I go out to eat I'll catch some fire ants from my backyard and put them in a vial. It's important that the ants are alive, so make sure you use a vial with a tight cap so they don't escape. I use a cool little spy gizmo that looks just like a pen but has a secret airtight compartment in the back, presumably to hide drugs.

"Anyway, I'll order a really nice meal with wine and whatnot, and then will order some sort of darkish dessert, like chocolate cake or brownies, and ask for the check. Once the waiter leaves I'll pretend I'm signing the check with the pen but will actually dump the ants all over the dessert. Then I'll

Free "anniversary" desert from Il Mulino

quietly motion the waiter over and very calmly show him the ants. The reason it's important that it's a dark dessert is because any decent waiter is going to notice ants on ice cream or something as he's bringing it to your table, but not so much on a sticky dark cake-type of dessert.

"Usually the waiter is so appreciative that I'm not freaking out and causing a scene that he immediately suggests comp'ing my whole meal. Other times I'll have to raise my voice loud enough to get some of the other patrons to turn their heads, but yeah, that's as far as I've ever had to go with it. Never had to talk to a manager or anything like that.

"With bigger groups, when I know the bill is going to be pretty expensive, I'll put a roach in a contact lens case with a little water so it doesn't dry out. Then I'll order a drink and when I'm almost completely done with the drink I'll pretend I'm having problems with my contacts and dump the roach in. Then I pull the same trick with the waiter. Usually I try to not even let the other people at the table know what's going on. The roach trick also works well in salads and pastas, but in that case you really have to give up at least half of your meal for it to work, because nobody is going to believe you ate your whole meal and found a roach at the very bottom, whereas that's exactly what would happen with a drink."

"That's pretty fucked up, Dan," I say, not able to hide my contempt.

"Sure it is, but I've probably saved thousands in meals over the years, and I can eat wherever I want and order whatever I want without worrying about being able to afford it." He smiles. "From my perspective, you're the one who's fucked up for paying crazy Disney prices for your meals."

"I can't argue with you there," I sigh.

"Let's go to Narcoossee's," yells Dan, pulling out his spy pen. "My treat!"

Here are some more cheap food options:

- ❤ Bring food from home. Since Southwest lets each passenger check two bags, why not stuff one with non-perishable snacks like boxes of Cheese-Its, candy, and cookies? I'd also highly recommend bringing your own coffee, too, since there are only a handful of places in WDW to get decent java (the French Press at Jiko comes to mind). If you have a coffee maker in your room, the little airtight single-serving bags work great, and the new Starbucks VIA instant mixes are nice if you don't have a coffee maker or like drinking it on the go all day long.

- ❤ Get carry-out delivered to your room. If you were at home and you wanted pizza, what would you do? You'd call out for delivery! Well, there are plenty of places that will deliver to the resorts. Obviously WDW doesn't advertise this because they'd much rather you order their outrageously overpriced room service, but if you ask at the front desk they will give you a stack of menus from "authorized" restaurants. This can save you a ton of cash!

  My favorite food delivery at WDW is by far Giordano's Pizza. Up until recently there was no place to get decent pizza at WDW (Via Napoli somewhat changed this), so I was forced to seek out local delivery places to get my fix. Turns out that I hit a home run with this place, because not only do they deliver right to your resort, but they make an amazingly tasty and authentic Chicago-Style pie. The Large size weighs as much as a stack of bricks and can literally feed a family of 4 for at least three nights. Plus, if you do a Google search you can find a coupon for a free order of their delicious Tomato Basil Cheese Bread. Yum! The only annoying thing about Giordano's is that the two local locations (Kissimmee and Lake Buena Vista) seem to randomly decide which one of them is responsible for delivering to WDW Resorts. You might get the runaround at first but with a little coaxing either one will deliver. Even with a decent tip for the driver this is a helluva deal for the amount of food you get.

♥ As of this writing Restaurant.com offers discounted gift certificates for Garden Grove, Kimonos, Todd English's bluezoo, Il Mulino, and Shula's in the Swan/Dolphin resorts, and House of Blues at Downtown Disney. At various times throughout the year Restaurant.com will offer discount codes that let you get a $25 gift certificate for $1! There are some restrictions, like sometimes you have to spend over $35, or sometimes you have to get two entrees, but as a whole these are amazing deals and you can literally cut the cost of your meals in half just by using this website!

Grocery Delivery and Fridge Swaps Gone Wrong:

Here's the biggest money-saving tip of all: Order groceries and have them delivered to your room! There are currently two companies that perform this service: Wegoshop (http://www.wegoshop.com) and Garden Grocer (http://www.gardengrocer.com). While I've heard good things about both I tend to use Wegoshop because they'll clip and use coupons without being asked and will also pick out whatever brand of any given item is cheapest, whereas at Garden Grocer you have to choose specific items from their list at a set (inflated) price. We usually order breakfast foods like bagels and cream cheese, as well as a ton of mozzarella sticks, single-serving bags of chips and vegetables, and bottled water for bringing to the parks. Yes, you are allowed to bring food into the parks in soft-sided coolers, and that's good because spending $3 for a bottle of water is insane, and the water from the fountains tastes like it was filtered through a dirty diaper. I always freeze the bottles of water the night before which makes them act as ice packs to keep the cooler cold, and also gives you ice-cold water throughout the day which is a huge relief during the scorching summers.

But the best thing about grocery delivery is that they will deliver booze! This alone usually makes up ¾ of my bill from Wegoshop, because I absolutely love coming back to the room at night and relaxing on the balcony with a few cold beers. And then I come inside and lie on the bed and watch Stacey running through all of the parks, being perkily annoying (her last name is Aswad!) yet somehow hot (especially in a bikini and pigtails during the Typhoon Lagoon section), and I'll have a few more beers. And then I'll sit in the Jacuzzi and drink some more beer. And then I'll go to sleep, but not before having another beer. I'm on vacation, dammit! As you can imagine, if I bought this much beer from WDW I'd be out of cash the first day of the trip, so the grocery delivery places are a godsend. I also know people who buy margarita mix and bottles of tequila from Wegoshop, mix the margaritas in their room, poor it all into a large thermos, and bring it to the pool for a relaxing day of poolside drunkenness.

Tip: If you do run out of alcohol from the grocery delivery place (or never ordered it to begin with and are rapidly running out of cash) you can walk over to the Hess gas station across from The Boardwalk and buy beer for cheap there, although their selection sucks. There is also a Hess station across the street from Downtown Disney. You can take WDW buses to either DTD or The Boardwalk, and from experience even though the bus drivers will give you dirty looks when you hop on board with a case of Heineken, they won't stop you from getting on.

Of course, grocery delivery assumes you've taken my advice and are staying in a swank DVC room, and thus have at least a fridge, coffee maker, toaster, and microwave to store and reheat your leftovers, snacks, and breakfast food. But maybe you're scared of renting points or just really love Pop Century, and you don't have any of that stuff in your room. Turns out you're not exactly out of luck: both the Value and Moderate resorts have microwaves and toasters available for communal use in the food courts, Moderates have fridges and coffee makers in the room, and if you're staying at a Value you can rent a fridge from Disney for $10/day, although that sort of defeats the purpose of trying to eat cheaply.

Or, you can participate in a "fridge swap" via an online forum like Disboards (in the Budget Board subforum). The way a fridge swap works is that a group of people staying at a particular resort in the near or distant future pool together $10 or so each to purchase a small fridge from Walmart, which is shipped to the resort, addressed to the first person in line for the swap, or picked up from the store if the person has rented a car. That person keeps the fridge for the length of their vacation and then brings it down to Luggage Services, where it is stored until the next person in the swap arrives and picks it back up (alternately, if the two families' trips overlap, they can make the swap in person using a luggage cart). This way, everyone in the swap gets a fridge for the length of their vacation for $10 total, instead of $10/day! Sometimes other small appliances are purchased and stored inside the fridge between swaps, such as toasters and coffee machines.

For the most part this works out really well; for whatever reason Disney hasn't cracked down on it yet, and Luggage Services seems to be more than happy to store and cart around heavy appliances as long as they get a decent tip. However, there have been fridge swaps gone wrong, resulting in some hilariously epic threads where a fridge gets lost (i.e., someone leaves it in their room without bothering to bring it back down to Luggage Services) and the rest of the people in the swap group who already chipped in for it get screwed. You'd think their firstborn had been kidnapped the way these swap participants freak the fuck out about a missing fridge! I've also heard reports of Luggage Services CMs who don't get tipped appropriately and then purposefully switch up fridges or damage them, resulting in mass confusion and chaos on the boards.

Also, as opposed to the fridges and coffee makers that come stock in the Moderates and Deluxes, the swap appliances don't get cleaned on a regular basis. And you never know what weird shit people store in their fridge or run through their coffee machines. I heard a story of one lady who cleaned her daughter's underwear in the coffee maker using shampoo because she didn't pack enough pairs and didn't feel like buying more at the gift store.

But this one takes the cake: I was heading back to my room one morning and started talking to a CM while waiting for an elevator. She looked really pissed off, which is rare at WDW, since some really bad shit has to go down for the CMs to break their façade of bliss.

"Tough morning?" I ask, holding a cup of coffee and staring at some really weird-looking stains on the CM's outfit.

"Um… no," she says, following my gaze down to the stains. She sees them and curses in Spanish.

I nod, a bit taken aback (I learned Spanish curse-words by imitating Mouth from "The Goonies" as a kid), but try not to show it. "What are those stains?" I ask. They're glistening in the overhead lights.

"You do not want to know!" she shouts, looking on the verge of a breakdown.

"Sure, I do!" I respond cheerfully. The stains look suspiciously like… Oh Christ. I figure it out before she says it.

"I open fridge someone leave in room, and it is filled with used…

condoms!" She chokes back a sob. "They fall on floor and spill everywhere, and I have to clean!"

"That's some fucked up shit, right there," I say, legitimately disgusted.

"Yes, I will quit!" She looks down and sighs. "No…. I won't quit."

I hand her $20. "I hope your day gets better."

Her face cracks a smile. When I get back to my room the next day there are at least a dozen towel animals placed all over the room.

SOUVENIRS AND MERCHANDISE

WDW Merch is a Rip-Off:

T-shirts shouldn't cost $30. There is no reason why anyone should pay $15 for a coffee mug. Yet, I'm consistently amazed when I walk into Mouse Gears at Epcot and see people queued up with piles of merchandise in their hands, waiting to massively overpay for moderate-to-low quality Disney-branded crap.

Just a few years ago WDW merchandise used to be so cool. Each park carried completely different products, and even individual stores had their own theme and neat stuff for sale that you could only get in that one store. Anyone remember the kick-ass Magic Store on Main Street? But now everything is pretty much the same no matter which park or store you're in. Just like the food, Disney has made all of their merch ultra-generic and bland so they can order larger quantities for cheaper and spread it out across all of their retail outlets all over the globe. But of course none of those volume savings are passed onto the consumer; instead prices are actually jacked up to almost laughable rates.

On the rare occasion I actually see something I really like at the parks I'll take a picture and order it when I get home. I've found 90% of that expensive crap significantly discounted on eBay, and I'm able to get a great deal on it by using a bidding sniper like the one at http://www.bidnip.com. If it can't be found on eBay oftentimes a wide variety of park merch is highly discounted at the Outlet section of Disney's own DisneyStore.com. At the very least I'll have to pay the same price as I would've at the parks but won't have to pay tax, will be able to use a coupon for free shipping, and will also get cashback by shopping through Mr Rebates (http://www. MrRebates.com). So if your kids just have to have those mouse ears in the parks, go ahead and order them ahead of time from DisneyStore.com, get the cashback, and avoid waiting in yet another line during your vacation.

Tip: Cast Members get up to 40% off merchandise! This rate fluctuates, and goes higher during the holidays, but it actually brings the prices down to a reasonable level. So, again, befriend a CM, give them some cash, and get them to buy a bunch of merch for you!

PhotoPass Shares:

One of the best mementos a family can take away from WDW is a set of photographs they can look at forever to relive their (hopefully) wonderful vacation. But the annoying thing about family photos is that you either have to bug a stranger to take the picture for you (thus risking an annoyed stranger, a shitty picture, and possibly a snatch and run camera theft) or someone from the family has to take the picture themselves and not be included in what might have otherwise been a perfect group photo for the mantle.

Luckily, Disney offers a service called PhotoPass which solves this problem: they hire photographers to roam the most picturesque spots in the parks, just waiting to take a once-in-a-lifetime picture of you, your wife, your eight kids and grandkids, and Crazy Uncle Billy, who just got out of prison and will probably be back there a month from now, all smiling in front of Cinderella's Castle.

The first time you run into one of these well-marked (they're almost always wearing khaki vests) if not exactly well-trained photographers they will hand you a plastic card with a number on it. Every time you want a picture, you hand that same card to the photographer, they take your picture, and then they scan the card. Everybody in the family can get their own card, too, in case you get sick of Crazy Uncle Billy and decide to strike off on your own and get Photopass pictures of you drinking various alcoholic beverages around the world at Epcot. Then when you get home you type each card number into http://www.DisneyPhotoPass.com and all of the pictures from your entire vacation are there for you to preview! You can then edit the photos, delete incriminating ones, add fancy borders and other such nonsense, and then have them all put on a CD and shipped to you!

Unfortunately, in typical Disney fashion they also charge out the ass for this service. Regardless of how many pictures you actually had taken, the cost is still about $120 for the CD. So if you only had eight pictures taken, and only one was actually in focus and properly exposed by the decidedly amateur-level photographer, you're going to pay $120 for that one picture. Conversely, if you were there for a month and had 800 pictures taken, it still costs $120 for the CD (or multiple CDs if needed). The only catch is that you need to enter your card numbers within 30 days of having the pictures taken, and then you have 30 days after that to order your photos.

Hopefully you're starting to see how this system is ripe for exploitation. Some brilliant Dark-Sider realized that if a) you can enter as many cards as you want into the PhotoPass site, and b) they'll send you as many pictures as you want, then c) multiple families visiting within a 30-day period can type their card numbers into the site and share a single CD. And thus was born the "PhotoPass Share"!

I use TourGuideMike.com for my PhotoPass shares, but they're organized on any number of WDW fan boards. The way it works is that someone becomes an "owner" for a particular group, meaning that this person will be the one who purchases the CD, makes copies of the CD for everyone in the group, and mails out the copies. Then people sign up for a particular group, depending on when they'll be visiting WDW. Once there are enough people signed up (usually up to 10 families) the group is closed and everyone sends in the money for the PhotoPass pre-order via check or PayPal, the cost of which is split equally between the families. It usually ends up costing about $20 per family, which is a huge discount over the initial price and actually makes this service a bargain! When each family gets back from vacation they type their code into the site and wait. Once all of the families in the group have come home and entered their codes the "owner" orders the CD, makes copies, and sends out the copies to everyone in the group! The only downside is that you end up with a CD full of pictures of people you've never met before, but sometimes that ends up being interesting in a voyeuristic sort of way.

HAVING FUN WITHOUT SPENDING A DIME

Did you know that you could have an entirely fun-filled vacation at Walt Disney World without ever setting foot in the parks? While this isn't something Disney advertises (because they want you to spend a ton of cash on park tickets), the resorts in particular offer enough amenities to make even the most jaded traveler squeal like an infant. Hell, you don't even have to stay at one of the resorts to take advantage of some of these activities; just stay at a fleabag offsite, make a dining reservation at your favorite resort, and then drive over and park there!

I've had many fun days just going around to the various WDW resorts, checking out the architecture, visiting their restaurants and food courts, and getting completely blasted at the various themed bars. The busses can take you from any park to any resort, or if you don't want to buy park tickets you can use Downtown Disney as a hub for catching busses to the resorts. Alternately you can do "themed" tours, such as the Resort Monorail tour of The Contemporary, Polynesian, and Grand Floridian, or walk around the Epcot Resorts (Yacht and Beach Clubs, Boardwalk, and The Swan and Dolphin).

Here are my Resort Hopping highlights:

Monorail Bar Crawl:

There are some massively awesome bars on the Resort Monorail loop at The Magic Kingdom, and if you start at around 6PM you can work in a whole night of boozing that rivals any hotspot nightclub locale on the planet.

I like to start at The Wave in The Contemporary. Over to the right side of the restaurant there's a super-cool blue-lit area that is something straight out of Star Trek. If you time it right you can go from there to the bar at The California Grill and watch the Magic Kingdom's fireworks. Disregard what everyone says about this place: you do NOT need to check in at the lobby to get access to this restaurant. Just take the elevator up to the 15th floor, walk past the host/ess, and take a seat at the bar. Order some sushi while you're at it!

After that it's over to The Polynesian for tiki drinks at The Tambu Lounge! This place is crowded earlier in the evening with people waiting for their reservations at Ohana's, which is right next door. But after the fireworks it clears out a bit and you can sit back with a Mai Tai in a shelled-out pineapple (the Lapu Lapu) and listen to a Don Ho impersonator while eating tasty appetizers. Heaven. And if you want, you can even take your drink out to the beach and watch the waves lap against the sand while you lap up some more rum concoctions.

The final stop is Mizner's Lounge at The Grand Floridian. Wind down with one of their fine ports while listening to the big band or lobby pianist. This place looks a little stuffy, but don't let that stop you; there's a great view of the GF gardens, and most importantly (and rare for WDW) FREE MOTHERFUCKING NUTS! As long as you're ordering their overpriced drinks don't be shy about requesting more and more nuts!

Unfortunately, Mizner's, along with the rest of the WDW bars, closes at 12AM. So if you're still in a party mood at that time you're going to have to go elsewhere. Fuckers.

A Mai Tai from the Tambu Lounge at The Polynesian

Free Boat Rides:

For some reason, even though I'm not a big fan of going boating in the ocean, I absolutely love riding around in the boats at WDW. And luckily, most of those boat rides are free, and very scenic. Two in particular are pretty outstanding. First is the Sassagoula River Cruise from Port Orleans to Downtown Disney. It's nice and long (2.5 miles – about 25 minutes), goes past a lot of woods (and the new Treehouse Villas), isn't choppy at all, and there aren't a ton of stops to break the calm (just one at French Quarter).

The second is the ride from The Magic Kingdom to The Wilderness Lodge. It's a little choppier since it's on a lake and not a canal, but during this ten minute ride you get to see up-close a lot of Bay Lake that you'd never get to see otherwise unless you rented some sort of watercraft. The big plus of this boat ride is that you get dropped off at a very quaint and rustic dock with a lovely walking trail to the backside of The Wilderness Lodge, which is fun to explore in and of itself (especially the geyser and hot springs).

Pool Hopping:

Why bother paying $50 to get into Typhoon Lagoon when there are bunch of resorts full of kick-ass pools, lazy rivers, and water slides available for free? Each of the resorts has multiple pool areas, and each has one "themed" pool. It's not really fair to say that the Deluxe resorts have more interesting or better themed pools than the Moderates or Values, because they're all pretty cool. However, Stormalong Bay, the water area at The Yacht and Beach Club, definitely takes the cake with its sandy bottom, lazy

The lazy river at Stormalong Bay

river, and a slide that goes through the broken mast of a shipwrecked boat.

Of course, "pool hopping", as it's known, is not technically allowed by Disney. You're only allowed to do this if you're a DVC member. However, the only place where they actively check your room key to see if you're staying at the resort is Stormalong Bay. And to be honest, there are so many entrances to Stormalong Bay that it's easy to bypass this "security". For example, the simplest way to completely get around Stormalong Bay's key-checkers is to start your visit with a ride on the slide! Yep, just climb the stairs to the slide, go down the slide, and BAM, you're in like Flynn. They do give you a wristband to wear, but just tell them it was pulling on your arm hair so you took it off. Alternately, you can buy a pack of multicolored Tyvek armbands at Party City, look to see what color they're giving out that day, and slap one on!

I've never had anyone check for a room key at any of the other pools, although technically it's possible, I suppose. But if you tell them that you're there for a meal and decided to swim beforehand, I seriously doubt they're going to kick you out, because they want your money!

The shipwreck slide at Stormalong Bay

Path from the Epcot area to the shipwreck slide, down into Stormalong Bay

Probably the best area to pool hop if you don't have a car, aside from the Stormalong Bay/Boardwalk combo (creepy clown slide at The Boardwalk!) is the Monorail Resort loop, where you have quick access to at least one awesome pool (the volcano @ The Polynesian) and two pretty decent although less exciting pools at The Contemporary and The Grand Floridian, all within minutes of each other via the monorail Resort loop. Get bored at one, and just hop on the monorail and go to another one!

However, if you have a rental car and don't mind using it, you could easily spend two days visiting all of the resort pools (and their associated waterside bars!) and having a helluva time going down all of the different slides, sitting in the hot tubs, and just generally enjoying life!

2

Sex, Drugs, & Rock 'n Roll at WDW

When you think of Walt Disney World, the first things that come to mind probably aren't sex, drugs and rock and roll. In fact, Disney has gone to great lengths to remove any traces of the party lifestyle from the parks, be it by shutting down Pleasure Island, dress code restrictions for cast members (including limitations on makeup and jewelry), a ban of alcohol sales in The Magic Kingdom, and just generally catering towards G/PG kid-oriented entertainment. But if you know where to look, you just might find, you'll get what you need....

SEX

Given that sex is one of those basic human needs, like food, shelter, and beer, if you're an adult vacationing at WDW, chances are at some point you're either going to have sex with your partner, or if you're single, you'll be looking for someone to hook up with. And we're not talking about romance here; numerous books have already covered Disney romance in depth. No, we're talking about good old-fashioned bumping and grinding in The Happiest Place on Earth.

So what carnal opportunities does Disney offer to those of us who see Snow White or Prince Charming (or for the Furries out there, Miriam from Robin Hood) as carnal objects of lust?

First, let's focus on those who go to the land with a partner. Assuming you're not too worn down by a day of commando park touring, there are plenty of wonderful places in and around the parks for some seriously awesome shagging.

At the Resorts:

This is a given, especially if you have a 1 or 2 bedroom at one of the DVC properties (hot tub!). The beds are super comfortable (you did check for bedbugs, right?) and while the walls are a bit thin and you might get some complaints if you're knocking boots all hours of the night, the privacy factor is definitely a plus for the more conservative folks out there. Of course, you can still be a little daring in your room, since the deluxe resorts all have lovely balconies, perfect for a semi-public snog. Blowjob while watching the Illuminations fireworks? Multitasking at its finest! But come on, you can have sex in a hotel room anywhere in the world. You're in Disney, live a little!

Elsewhere at the resort hotels:

Most of the deluxe resorts have plenty of secluded spots, from the beaches of The Grand Floridian and the Yacht and Beach Club to wooded alcoves at The Wilderness Lodge and Treehouse Villas, but The Polynesian takes the cake. With tropical plants, waterfalls, and a cool breeze coming off of Bay Lake, the Polynesian might be the biggest man-made aphrodisiac ever created. There are literally dozens of beautiful secluded spots here, be it on the beach or in the midst of some greenery. If this place can't get your blood pumping you're probably dead. This author has brought numerous dates there, and sitting on a swing at the beach, watching the fireworks and the Electric Light Parade has always managed to seal the deal.

Great place to watch the Wishes fireworks. . . while having sex

Prime Polynesian spot for nighttime sex

Another popular spot for public fornication at the resorts seems to be the hot tubs at the pools. Personally, this seems a bit disgusting, not so much for you, but for the poor person who gets in there after you've finished your business. Show some respect for your fellow vacationers, people!

Just no. . . Don't have sex here.

Finally, a secret spot. Don't tell anybody. If you've ever been lucky enough to eat at the California Grill on the 15th floor of The Contemporary, you probably know that you can see the fireworks at The Magic Kingdom perfectly from the windows. But did you know that there's another, more private viewing area on that same floor? Follow the corridor to the right of the elevator down to a set of doors. The doors open to a huge outside balcony that nobody visits except to watch the fireworks at MK. Sex as the monorail glides under your feet is quite the experience. Tip: if there are people on that level, you can simply take the outside stairway to the next balcony down, which offers the same view and is actually even more secluded.

Any 4 of these balconies are prime sex spots

The hallway from California Grill to the balconies

The top right balcony - note the incredible view of MK

The balcony below, looking over to the opposite side

In the Parks:

By definition, if you're having sex in one of the parks you're having sex in public, which is illegal and if you're caught will likely get you thrown out and possibly arrested. Also be aware that the majority of the rides in the World are almost 100% monitored by cameras. Now, while that will excite the hardcore exhibitionists out there, some of you might not appreciate the fact that a pimply-faced cast member and all of his friends will be using a video copy of your escapades as spank material. Finally, there are kids everywhere! Be discrete, and don't traumatize some poor child for life because you decided it would be fun to hump Goofy's leg. Not cool!

With those caveats out of the way, sex in the parks is a unique experience that you simply can't replicate anywhere else. How many places can you orgasm while staring at a fairly accurate replica of Johnny Depp or Abraham Lincoln (who, believe it or not, is actually the subject of an entire subset of fetishists)?

So without further adieu, here are the best places in the parks to get your move on (sometimes quite literally!), in order of safest to you-must-love-jail craziest.

1. Companion restrooms. Essentially these are meant for parents to go into with their too-young-for-adult-restroom kids, but they're also a perfect place to go with your partner. Yes, I know, "ick!" But the restrooms at Disney are notoriously clean, especially these ones, since not many people go into them. Plus, there's a lock on the door and no cameras, assuring that you won't get caught. The best of these seem to be at Epcot, although they can be found at any of the parks.

Might as well say "Sex Room"

The very clean and spacious Companion Restroom in Mexico

2. Carousel of Progress. At certain times of the year this quaint animatronic show is virtually empty, and there are no cameras in the theater. Sit in the back and go for third base in a dark, air-conditioned theater as the robots lull the rest of the audience to sleep.

    A while back a fellow Dark-sider told me how he actually walked up the ramp with a date, opened the door, and found the whole ride empty. "We went up to the theater but nobody was there to let us in. We saw that one of the doors on the far left side was cracked, so we walked in and it was empty and dark. Not sure if it was down for repairs, or what. The stage was locked on the "modern" scene, the curtain was up, and the whole family was there, looking like they were taking a nap (the dog looked dead, to be honest). So we went up onstage and did it right behind dad in the kitchen, knowing that he could wake up at any time! It was like being back in high

Completely empty theater during a showing of Carousel of Progress

school, trying to sneak one past our parents or something. Pretty exciting!"

3. FutureWorld East at Night. Universe of Energy closes way earlier than any of the other rides in FutureWorld (because it's a 40 minute show), and for most of the year The Wonders of Life Pavilion isn't even open (and when it is open it's totally dead at night). After dark during the shorter days of the year this area is nearly abandoned, and between these two pavilions there is a large section of welcoming foliage you can venture back into and recreate your own XXX version of the opening scenes from the now defunct "Making of Me".

4. Tom Sawyer's Island. There are a ton of dark, secluded spots here, especially in Injun Joe's Cave (The Mining Cave has NO secluded spots!). But be forewarned that kids are swarming in the busy months as their parents let them run wild to burn off excess energy. So your chances of getting caught rise exponentially as the crowd levels increase. Best to go here towards the end of the day.

Without the flash, this Future World East location is dark and secluded at night

5. The monorail from The Magic Kingdom to Epcot is also ideal for a quickie, especially during those Evening Magic Hours that last until 2AM (so the monorail runs until 3AM). Find an empty cabin and go at it. Don't believe me? Check out http://www.flashmountain. com/monorail-girl.php for pictures of a girl totally nude on the WDW monorail; there's even a video you can order for only $9.95! Totally worth it, btw. In this video, it initially looks like there are other people in the cabin, and there are even sound effects added so that it sounds like a large crowd is are in there. But subsequent shots show that for the most graphic parts the cabin was empty, and two separate trips were cut together. Looks like this was done in the middle of the day, but it would obviously work anytime you can find an empty cabin.

6. The secret trail in Animal Kingdom. There is one particular trail around the giant phallic symbol known as The Tree of Life that

Entrance to Injun Joe's Cave

Flash-illuminated sex hidaway - even has a seat for comfort!

MONORAIL GIRL!!!

Entrance to secret trail via exit of "Tough to be a Bug"

The secret AK trail

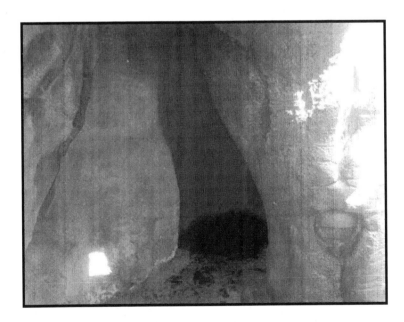

A flash-illuminated sex hideaway on the AK trail

it seems nobody knows about, probably because the entrance and exit aren't really marked. To get to the trail, go through the Fastpass area for A Bugs Life. You'll find the trail on the left side. The warnings here are the same as for Tom Sawyer's Island, so play it safe!

7. Journey Into Your Imagination. A few sources in the know claim that there are no cameras on this ride, much like there weren't in the long defunct Horizons ride. Since Journey has been butchered into a boring shell of its former self, there's really nothing better to do on this ride than have some "imaginative" sex.

Nobody rides this thing, might as well have sex

8. The Utilidors at MK or Backstage at Epcot. "Wait, what?!" you gasp. "You're not even supposed to be there to begin with! How is this a good place to have sex?" Well, as far as gaining access to the tunnels or backstage, read the tips and tricks later in the book. Once you get there and realize nobody gives a shit, you'll find a massive network of tunnels at MK with dozens of forgotten storage rooms, and all sorts of strange abandoned hideaways at Epcot where you

should have no trouble finding a private spot to get your groove on.

9. Any of the dark rides, especially Haunted Mansion and Pirates of the Caribbean. Look, you're just asking for trouble here. There are cameras everywhere, and if you're even so much as making out you'll hear a cast member telling you over the speakers to cut it out. If you persist, they'll stop the ride and escort you out. But I'm sure some of you are going to do it anyway, so if you do, be as discrete as possible, hopefully settling for a handy or fingerbang under a jacket.

Example of one of the camera monitoring stations at WDW

A cast member tells the story of how he was working evening EMH hours at Mansion, around 1:30AM. "A couple came in giggling, and they were the only people who'd come in for at least five minutes so they had the ride all to themselves. We knew pretty much right away what was going to happen, so after they got on the ride we kept our eyes glued to the cameras. They put on the craziest XXX-rated show we'd ever seen! It's not like you can do it in a normal position in the ride vehicles anyway, but they were all over the place! When they got off the ride we all stood there and gave them a round of applause. The girl was blushing like crazy but the guy seemed to love it and gave us all high-fives!"

10. Honorable mention: Skyway. Oh, Skyway, how we miss you! Although this ride doesn't exist anymore (supposedly closed for engineering reasons, although popular consensus is that it was a safety hazard since you could literally jump to your death), it was a mecca for the horny. No cameras, on top of the crowd so nobody could see you, but still out in the open air. The number of kids conceived up here over the years must have been staggering.

So there you go, the best places in Walt Disney World to have sex! Take that, Fodors!

To deviate (no pun intended) slightly from the topic, another sex-related ride "must do" is showing your boobs on Splash Mountain, better known to cast members as "Flash Mountain". Right as you go down the climax of the ride (a huge waterfall) a hidden camera snaps your picture, which you can then purchase on your way out. Apparently it's become something of a rite of passage for women to bare their breasts right at this moment, camera be damned. Of course, since it's Disney, they've devised a protocol to shelter young eyes from this behavior, and have set the camera system on a 35 second time delay so that they can quickly block any photos with bare breasts from appearing on the big screen at the photo kiosk.

However, it seems as if some enterprising cast members have figured out a way to shift these pix to some other form of storage, and have graciously posted them for all to see at http://www.flashmountain.com/spl.php!

How to Find Someone to Have Sex With:

If you're single and on the prowl, let's be honest: WDW probably isn't the best vacation spot for random hookups. Go to Cancun or Daytona if that's all you're interested in. However, if you're mainly looking for a fun and memorable vacation, with a little tail on the side, that can definitely be arranged.

Cast Members:

Throughout the year the parks are staffed by college students there for the College Program, where horny teenagers from all over the world come to work for a pittance, both because they love Disney, and because it looks pretty good on a resume. As of this writing, there were 8,000 students working for the Mouse each year via this program, with 4,000 on site at any given time!

The majority of these young cast members are placed in menial positions, such as serving/cooking food or cleaning bathrooms, so anything you can do to make their day a little brighter will definitely make you stand out from the throngs of irritable and annoying guests they usually deal with. If you see an attractive young cast member, by all means chat them up and see if you can get invited back to one of their off-site housing complexes (i.e., dorms) where all of the typical hijinks often associated with college housing occur on a daily basis. These apartments are definitely party central for college-age cast members, and getting invited here on a weekend is like hitting the mother load for a single looking for a hookup at WDW.

"It really is like a freshman dorm," says a young female DCP attendee. "People have to work shitty shifts at all hours and all days of the week, and it's tough to have a normal social life outside of the program. So everyone just hooks up with everyone else in the apartment complex; it's very incestuous. After a few weeks we realized that the boys in the program were super immature, so my friends and I were definitely on the prowl in the parks for attractive guys. Since most guests treated us like crap, anyone who was even remotely nice stood out from the crowd. I'd give nice guys FastPasses with my number written on the back."

Here's an extra special tip: try to get invited to The Commons, which is where the international cast members live. For The World Showcase in Epcot, Disney tries to hire students who are actually from the countries represented in the individual pavilions, both to create an authentic experience for guests, and also so that the international cast members feel a little more comfortable in their environment, given that most of them are in the US for the first time.

As has been shown in numerous studies over the years, many other countries have much more liberal attitudes towards sex than the US does, so odds are that you have a better chance of a one-night stand with these cast members. Specifically, Scandanavian countries rank high on the promiscuity scale (and are also very friendly towards LGBT lifestyles), so it would behoove you to head on over to World Showcase and start hitting on the cast members at Norway!

Hot Norway Cast Members!

For more information on cast member debauchery, I'd recommend *Mouse Tales* by David Koenig, *Cast Member Confidential* by Chris Mitchell, and Kevin Yee's *MouseTrap*.

Locals:

Unfortunately, one of the best spots to pickup locals is now shuttered. Pleasure Island was a strip of highly themed bars and dance clubs in the Downtown Disney area. The great thing about them is that you could easily pickup the type of person you were interested in by nature of the club that they frequented. If you wanted a good ole country boy or girl to line dance with, you went to the Wildhorse Saloon. If you wanted an 80s rock star with enough hairspray to punch a hole in the ozone layer you went to Rock N Roll Beach Club. BET Soundstage for the urban crowd, and 8Trax for the MILFs. Or the much celebrated Adventurers Club for the true Disney-aholics. These clubs were quite the experience, and definitely lent themselves to heavy drinking and random hookups, which is assumably why Disney shut them down. Major bummer!

As of the time of this writing, the closest thing to Pleasure Island is Universal's CityWalk. Of course, the issue here is that if you're staying onsite you either need to drive there (and thus probably drive home drunk, which is dumb), or take a cab, which is going to cost you a pretty penny. The fact that Disney has given up on such a major demographic and allowed their competition to take the reigns seems like a major blunder, but such criticism is moot at this point, and all we can do is hope that they eventually come to their senses.

So what we have left for nightlife at WDW are the Atlantic Dance Club and Jellyrolls, both located at The Boardwalk. I have never seen anybody in the Atlantic Dance Club. The place seems perpetually dead, even with no cover charge. Which, on a good night might actually work to your advantage since there would be less competition from other potential suitors. But it's hard to have fun in a dead club, because you just know that other people are having a better time than you are somewhere else. And Jellyrolls is great fun, but from experience it's not exactly a haven for singles.

At 9pm on Friday, Atlantic Dance Hall is completely empty

However, there is a ray of light at the end of the tunnel! Thanks to the Annual Pass, many locals come to Epcot's World Showcase on the weekends looking for a good time, much as you would at a local pub. This is especially prevalent during the Food and Wine Festival, where Epcot is literally overrun by locals getting their drink on. On the weekends it can get seriously sloppy here, and there are definitely some non-kid-friendly activities at hand. But again, think of this like a really huge bar, except with monster themeing (and much more expensive drinks), and it becomes pretty apparent that this is a good time and place to work your pickup artist magic.

Crowded World Showcase during Food & Wine Festival

Organized Singles Meet-Ups:

It turns out that there are hundreds, if not thousands of singles who LOVE all things Disney and go on solo trips to the Orlando parks on a fairly regular basis. The problem is that they're scattered across the globe and as of this writing there are no "Singles Days" at WDW like there are "Gay Days". But thanks to the magic of Al Gore's Interwebs it is super easy to schedule meet-ups online, not only at the parks, but in your own city!

The prime location for finding out about these meet-ups is on the venerable Disboards.com, in their "Disney for Adults/Singles" subforum. This is a wonderland outlet for those who want to schedule hookups, as not only are there threads organized by month for when singles will be visiting The World, but there is also what amounts to a Personals thread where people post their stats, specs, and pictures. Peruse through this board and you're bound to find someone who matches your type. Shoot them a PM and chat a bit offline, and then simply schedule a meeting place during your trip!

The great thing about WDW is that it's one of the safest places on earth for meeting strangers, and as previously mentioned there are a lot of great spots that are natural aphrodisiacs. While nobody is guaranteeing that you're going to find your perfect mate, the sounds, smells, and excitement of the parks are definitely conducive to getting people in the mood for lovemaking.

There are also meet-ups centralized to other geographic regions, with the most activity in the Baltimore/DC area. Now, far be it from this author to lecture anyone on the ways of love, but these meetings are obviously geared more towards people looking for a life-partner, not random hookups. So don't be surprised if you go into these events looking for a quick roll in the hay and are scorned and shot down like you just entered Westworld on the day when the computers malfunctioned. Because, let's be honest here, eating crabs in Baltimore is a far cry from sipping Grand Mariner slushies in France at the World Showcase, and while your lesser traits might be overlooked in the glittering lights of Illuminations, that comb-over isn't going to seem quite so charming as you stare down at the trash floating in the Inner Harbor.

Alternative Lifestyle Activities:

No, not Gay Days. Gay Days is no longer "alternative". It's just a happier, more brightly colored crowd than normal. No, if you're looking for something really wacky to do with your body on a WDW vacation, you're not going to find it in the parks. So rent a car, or better yet find a hot CM to drive you, and head on over to these two off-site wonderlands.

Cypress Cove Nudist Resort and Spa
http://www.cypresscoveresort.com

Did you ever notice that a lot of the Disney characters don't wear clothes, or even weirder, only wear tops? That's because Walt Disney was a strong proponent of nudism* (*this is blatantly false). So why not celebrate his achievements at a "clothing optional" nude beach where you can either be a creepy voyeur and gawk at saggy naked people while fully clothed, or join in the fun and gawk at saggy naked people while they also gawk at your sagginess. Yes, there is a bar, so go ahead and get liquored up and let it all hang out, just like Pluto!

Cypress Cove is about a 35 minute drive from WDW property. To get there, take Hwy 192 East to Poinciana Boulevard. Turn right and follow south for thirteen miles to Pleasant Hill Road. Turn left and go one-quarter mile to their gate, on the right.

The best part is that as of this writing, if you've never been to Cypress Cove before there's a coupon on their website that'll get you a tour of the place and all day admission for free! Couples-only, though – they don't let single guys in the door unless you can prove you've had a bunch of prior nudist-camp experience, which means having an expensive membership somewhere, which means you're at least a rich pervert.

Hint 1: Their gym is your best chance of seeing actual hot nude people, because let's face it, they're at least trying to maintain appearances. Just saying....

Hint 2: Bring a towel to sit on. Nobody wants to sit down on a hot barstool and get their bare ass soaked with your bare ass's sweat drippings. Or maybe they do, but if that's the case they're going to have to go somewhere else and pay a lot more money, because Cypress Grove isn't for fucking perverts! Except voyeurs. And exhibitionists. And maybe pedophiles. But, you know, other than that, no perverts allowed!

Orlando Love Loft
http://www.orlandoloveloft.com

Whereas, perverts of all sorts are more than welcome at The Orlando Love Loft! But mostly swingers. Which is pretty hot, so I've decided it's not perverted. Even if there's candlewax on the nipples involved, it's still hot, and thus not perverted. Fuck you Middle America, I'm making my own rules!

From their stock response e-mail (i.e., a real person wouldn't respond to my requests for an interview):

INFO@orlandoloveloft.com

Thank you for your E-mail. Feel free to call us toll free at 1-866-738-3950.

On Friday and Saturdays emails may not get answered in time; due to attending to our guests, so please call to be sure your questions get answered.

LADIES ARE ALWAYS FREE

What is the dress code? CASUAL

Do we have to become a member? NO

Is there any additional charge at the door?
COUPLE: $40
SINGLE MALE: $60
SINGLE FEMALE: FREE

Do you bring your own drinks? BYOB - Bring your own alcoholic beverages Coke, Diet Coke, Sprite and bottled water & munchies provided.

PARTY STARTS AT 8 PM TILL 2 AM

LOCATION: 8310 Happy Trails Rd, Kissimmee, FL 34747

Directions: I-4 to Exit 60 (SR 429 North) then Exit #1 (Sinclair) .25 cent toll. Turn left onto Sinclair, go over the bridge. Then Right on Happy Trails Then 1 mile to the address of 8310 Happy Trails kissimmee, Fl 34747 on the left. Drive in gate to parking area and enter the left of the house.

I don't know why, but when I think about this place, I always picture Jay from Kevin Smith's movies standing in the living room yelling, "I'm gonna fuck that bitch, and that bitch, and that one, too! Snoogins!" Not sure why I think the clientele there would act like that, but since the owners wouldn't fucking get back to me for an interview, I've decided to make gross generalizations based on my out-of-control imagination.

The Last Resort: (no, not the long-awaited Art of Animation Resort):

Ugh, it's come to this. After days of staring at Snow White, Cinderella, and/or Captain Jack, you are very, very, very horny. You've had no luck with disboards.com, Atlantic Dance Hall has been a predictable bust, and the language barrier with the Norway cast members was insurmountable. So you've decided to hire an escort.

For what it's worth, the escorts in the Orlando area are more attractive than average, and also charge much less than average, around $100 per hour as of this writing. This might be the only time on your WDW vacation where you're actually getting a bargain! And for a little extra, you might even be able to get them to dress up in that Prince Charming or Cinderella getup (or that Robin Hood furry costume if that's your thing) that you packed for just this very occasion.

It goes without saying, but you should do your research here. You don't want to be on the wrong end of this sort of business deal. Having the cops bust in on you at The Grand Floridian would be oh so gauche, and the height of bad manners. So it's highly recommended that you visit http://www.theeroticreview.com for reviews and pictures of the local escorts. Note that many of them only do incalls, so you'll need a taxi or rental car. Some do outcalls, but they cost more, although I would argue that it's worth the cost since you've already paid for the comforts of a WDW resort. And seriously, doing it in a crappy apartment or Super-8 would totally kill the magic.

DRUGS

Where to Score?:

Marijuana, Ecstasy, psychedelics and WDW are a wonderful

combination. The blacklight neon frenzy of Buzz Lightyear (I mean, c'mon, the fucking ride has the word "Buzz" in it!), the tranquil sights, sounds, and smells of Soarin', and the base humor of "Muppet Vision: 3D" all have the potential to be more fun when high on the right drug. And the message of peace, love, and harmony in "It's a Small World" is much more profound while stoned, assuming the music doesn't send you into a paranoid attack.

Used to be you could hold a stash of whatever in the crotch of your pants or elsewhere on your body when getting on a plane, but with the advent of the new full-body scanners that penetrate clothing, that's no longer possible. Anyone who gets on a plane holding illegal drugs is asking for a Federal felony offense for interstate drug trafficking, and that would be a lousy way to start a vacation.

So if you can't take it with you, you have to buy it there, and thus the question becomes: how does one score drugs at WDW?

Cast Members:

Aside from booze, which can be found in abundance anywhere in WDW aside from The Magic Kingdom, it appears that drugs are severely frowned upon onsite for anyone whose name isn't "Dopey". The website for the College Program states:

Disney has a zero-tolerance policy for drug use on Disney property, and this includes The Commons and Vista Way. Get caught using, selling, or possessing and you are terminated and sent home, and possibly arrested. Commons security will inspect apartments randomly and has the right to terminate anyone who is caught with drugs in their apartment - and even their roommates! The Company does not have a testing policy, but naturally reserves the right to do so.

Reading between the lines, what this means is that there is no initial drug testing done in order to be admitted to the CP, but if you're caught with it while you're there, you're immediately fired. I've confirmed this with several former CP alums, who also told me that it's fairly common for CP CMs to solve rivalries by reporting their enemies to the Disney drug police. So unless a CP member plans on being friends with everyone, keeping drugs onsite is a big risk.

I've also talked to numerous "lifer" CMs about this, and not one has been able to give me a reliable source for scoring marijuana, ecstasy, or any other mid-level drugs on property. It was suggested to me that those looking for drugs at the parks talk to a busboy or janitor, i.e., someone with a lower-level position. But that's basically a crapshoot, and if you talk to the wrong person you could get kicked out of the park for such inquiries.

Off Property:

Per Hoot Gibson, our intrepid Horizons urban explorer: "The easiest way [to get pot offsite] is to drive your rental car to International drive and buy it by the bale. Near Wet and Wild. I don't smoke it but if you're in town and looking for it I know 150 people ready to sell:)"

LOL, thanks, Hoot!

Another suggestion I received from a former (now reformed) Orlando dealer: "Right now, I bet 25% of the people at Austin's and Stardust are high." Looking into it, both of these are Orlando coffee shops that are hippy/alternative hangouts (http://www.austinscoffee.com/ and http://www.myspace.com/stardustvideoandcoffee). Stardust in particular sells vegan food and has a drink called "The Stoner"... so, yeah, not a bad bet you can score there.

Having Friends:

And as usual, your best bet is to have some actual friends in Orlando who already know people they can buy from. So maybe get on Facebook and reconnect with old friends or start talking to people on message boards (that shit won't fly on Disboards, but try http://forums.wdwmagic.com/ or http://theunoriginaldistroublemakersclub for more liberal forumites). If you're not an asshole or a narc, in all likelihood you can utilize your social network to get your OWN guy in Orlando, and buy from him/her whenever you're in town.

How to Safely Get High in the Parks:

Getting high in your hotel room isn't much of a risk at all, especially if you're using a vaporizer. But buzzing in your hotel isn't much different than doing it at home, and what's the fun in that? No, what you really want is the experience of being completely blasted in the Parks! Unfortunately Disney doesn't make this easy. There are an unknown number of undercover security agents patrolling the parks, dressed like tourists. If you're stone cold sober and very observant it's pretty easy to pick them out of the crowd, but if you're in an "altered state" it's going to be tough and you don't want to risk blazing up in front of one of them.

And if you get caught with drugs in the parks you're not just getting kicked out. Nope, chances are you're also getting hit with a felony charge, not a simple misdemeanor because of a Florida law that allows for stiffer penalties if drugs are found within 100 ft of the presence of minors. So even getting caught for possession of a small amount of marijuana could get you busted for a 2nd degree felony. Furthermore, since you're likely from out of state you could get arrested for trafficking, which is another felony.

So what to do if you want to get high in the parks? Here are some tips:

- Smoke it in the car in the parking lot before you enter the parks. Obviously this is the safest thing to do, but it also kinda sucks because by the time you get on the tram and actually into the park and on a ride, chances are your buzz is gone.
- Bake the weed into "Firecrackers", which are pot-infused peanut butter crackers. These will get past security with no problems and it'll just look like you're eating a snack, even though within an hour you'll have a massive buzz. Here's a recipe:

1. Grind up 1g of pot. You want a really fine grind to increase the surface level of the pot so more THC can be released.

2. Mix 2tbs of high-fat peanut butter (like the natural organic stuff with the liquid on top) with 2 tsp of vegetable oil. THC absorbs in oil, so adding this additional oil increases the potency.

3. Stir in the weed with the peanut butter/oil mixture.

4. Spread an even layer of this mix onto crispy crackers or tortilla chips (you want non-porous crackers so that they don't absorb the oil).

5. Place another cracker on top of each, and then wrap them all in aluminum foil.

6. Bake at 310-320 degrees (THC will be destroyed any higher than 340) for about 20 minutes.

7. Let cool and eat!

❦ This my favorite method. Buy a pouch of hand-rolled tobacco along with some filtered cigarette blanks and a blank filler (all of this should cost less than $10 at a tobacconist). Fill a bunch of blanks with an equal mixture of tobacco and finely ground weed. These end up looking just like regular cigarettes, and even better the tobacco masks the smell of the marijuana. So you can actually use these in the designated smoking areas at the parks and nobody will be the wiser!

❦ Final tip: Control your shit! If you get totally wasted and run around like an idiot you're going to attract attention and will likely get caught, searched for paraphernalia (yet another misdemeanor charge), and kicked out of the parks. Don't be like these guys: http://www.youtube.com/watch?v=7lu72WdTg2U

Top 5 Best and Worse Places to Get High:

I realize this is subjective, but there are just some experiences that are going to be awesome high, and others that are going to totally suck ass.

Best:

1. World Showcase at Epcot. When you've got the munchies there is no better place to be on this earth than at World Showcase. Sweet, sour, salty, chewy, crunchy, whatever, it's seemingly been placed here by the God of Stoners to appeal to the culinary desires of even the pickiest potheads. Plus, while you're eating you can totally chill and watch the waves on the lake or do the hippie twirling dance to a huge variety of music, from The Beatles to Japanese drums. I personally recommend the Biergarten restaurant in Germany – a lot of different types of fatty food combined with a show that will blow your fucking mind if you're stoned. There's a big horn duet, and two guys playing dueling bells, and lots of yelling. Awesomeness!

2. Soarin' at Epcot. Even when you're not stoned it feels like you're flying. Strike a fucking Superman pose and be a superhero for a few minutes or sit back and chill as the wind blows through your hair and scents of oranges, pines, and salt water waft through the air. A

full-body sensory experience that is transcendent when high.

3. Castaway Creek lazy river at Typhoon Lagoon. Totally chill and relaxing. You lay in a tube, stare up at the sky, and just… float.

4. The Many Adventures of Winnie the Pooh at The Magic Kingdom. You fly around watching Pooh desperately trying to get his honey fix. With the exception of Christopher Robin, who is a total prude, every character on this ride is stoned out of their gourds. There are blacklights and bright colors, a smooth, non-bumpy track, and lots of random shit going on. When Pooh finally gets his honey you will cry because you finally understand just what this poor little fucker goes through every day.

5. MuppetVision 3D at Disney Hollywood Studios. Henson was a stoner, and all of his creations, except maybe for Kermit and Piggy are on something. If you've never appreciated the Muppets, just watch this show high and be prepared to laugh your ass off the entire time.

Honorable Mention: Listen to the Land in Epcot. It's not a great ride, but the hydroponic setup should be inspiring for any pothead.

Worst:

1. Space Mountain at The Magic Kingdom. Just don't do it. You will freak the fuck out. You can't see shit, you're being thrown around, there are loud noises, and people are screaming. Talk about a total buzz kill!

2. Stitch's Great Escape at The Magic Kingdom. This is like the anti-Soarin'. They physically restrain you and then stick you in the dark while loud noises crash all around you and a horrible fart smell blasts out and then lingers for the rest of the show. Claustrophobia and paranoia ensues. Truly awful.

3. Dinosaur at Animal Kingdom. Fucking strobe lights, huge dinosaurs randomly jumping out at you and trying to eat your face, and a really bumpy and jerky ride makes for a bad trip. Plus, Phylicia Rashad is in there being a bitch, and you know she's putting on that Claire Huxtable face and judging you for being stoned just like she would with Theo.

4. Twilight Zone Tower of Terror at Disney Hollywood Studios. Look, you know the drop is going to happen at some point, so for the whole ride you're dealing with already freaky shit happening everywhere (like ghosts and shattering glass and Rod Serling floating around) so your paranoia just keeps building and building until you're having a full-on attack. And then when the drop does come, it's no relief because it drops a little, and you think it's over, and then it just goes back up again and drops again, over and over until you're having a heart attack. You will be a jittery paranoid mess for the rest of the day and you might have flashbacks and it will ruin your vacation.

5. It's a Small World. This might either fill you with joy and make you treasure world peace and cry about how beautiful the innocence of children is, or it will be the most excruciating ten minutes of your life. The "kids" are wooden figures with creepily limited movement, like something out of "Invasion of the Body Snatchers". And the song repeats over and over and over and drills into your head like a mantra and maybe permanently drives you insane like the lead character in "Franny and Zoey".

   Honorable Mention: Mission: Space at Epcot. The Orange line with the G-forces has killed quite a few people. This has nothing to do with being high, it just sucks.

ROCK N' ROLL

No, "High School Musical" doesn't count. Neither does "American Idol". "Rockin' Rollercoaster" is sorta kinda on the borderline. What I'm talking about is real, sexy, gritty rock at Walt Disney World. Is it possible? Does it exist? Surprisingly, the answer is "Yes!"

Rock Venues On-Site:

First up is the most obvious choice, The House of Blues in Downtown Disney. Most nights they have moderately priced mid-level acts in the venue next to the restaurant, so if you're not picky and don't mind spending $20 to see a show, you're pretty much guaranteed some decent rock music in a nice venue. They also sometimes have a guy playing acoustic guitar and singing in the bar out front of the restaurant, which simply isn't very rock n' roll, even if he does do watered down versions of 90s grunge hits.

Technically you can also hear rock songs at Jellyrolls on The Boardwalk, since when you tip the players you're allowed to request whatever song you want. Obviously you're only going to get a piano/vocal rendition, but it's pretty fun hearing these guys try to struggle through Black Dog or Enter Sandman on the piano. Worth a visit for the decidedly raucous crowd, even if the music is tame.

Food and Wine "Eat to the Beat":

Epcot's management brings in some lame ass acts for The Flower and Garden Festival in the spring (Jose Feliciano and Juice Newton are for old people). But in the fall for The Food and Wine Festival they pony up for some really great bands to play the "Eat to the Beat" series. Rick Springfield, 38 Special, Sister Hazel, Sugar Ray, Kool and the Gang, and Big Bad Voodoo Daddy are just some of the bigger acts that play at the lovely American Gardens Theater, across from the American Pavilion. If you line up early enough for each show you can easily get into the front row and have a much more intimate experience than you'll ever get in a stadium or even in most club settings. Better yet, the audio engineers are top notch, making sure everything sounds perfect and isn't destroying your eardrums. This provides a much more pleasurable concert than the typical wall of white noise you get elsewhere.

In fact, I've seen one of my more memorable rock shows in recent memory at Epcot: Night Ranger at F&W in 2009. Coming into it I thought they'd be pure cheese because all I really remembered was "Sister Christian", but these guys just tore it up and whipped the crowd into a frenzy during their last ½ hour set of the night. I know they're in their 50s, but they had more energy, stage presence, and love for what they were doing than 99% of the new rock bands I've seen. Made me into an instant fan, and reminded me of why I love rock n' roll!

That said, it's still Disney. Apparently during the 2009 "Eat to the Beat", young pianist and singer Vanessa Carlton said "fuck" once during her first set of her first day there. She apologized after being scolded by Disney, but then came out for her third set and said "fuck" again. Bam, gone. Booted the "fuck" out of Epcot and replaced with a local band. Apparently Disney

Night Ranger rocks Epcot's Eat to the Beat!

is okay with Billy Ocean singing about wanting to be someone's "Lover Boy" and Night Ranger's Joel Hoekstra sticking his tongue out at my wife and wiggling it in a manner simulating cunnilingus, but little innocent Vanessa Carlton can't say fuck. Sigh.

Nightly Epcot Acts:

If you can't make it for Food and Wine, there's also great rock music to be found on a daily basis at Epcot other times of the year. "The British Revolution" puts on five sets a night at the UK Pavilion, featuring a full spread of British Invasion tunes, from Queen to Zep to The Who and The Stones. While they don't dress up like their predecessors, "The British Invasion" (a Beatles tribute act), they're actually pretty fucking kick ass and heavier than anything else you're going to see at WDW. It's a real legit rock show! And true to form on the weekends it's virtually guaranteed that a sluttily dressed drunken groupie will be dancing lewdly in front of their bandstand, offending parents and scaring little children, until a DisCop kindly leads her out of the park.

Off Kilter, the kilt-wearing celtic rock band (who are incredible musicians) receive similar treatment from the ladies during their daily performances next to the Canada Pavilion, and I've even seen panties thrown up on stage during their gigs on crazier Food and Wine nights! Granted, the panties were thrown by overweight 50-somethings, but still... ROCK AND FUCKING ROLL AT DISNEY!!!

3

Assorted Tips, Tricks, Scams. . . and Bugs

TRICKS

Front of the Line With a Wheelchair:

People who say that being disabled at WDW doesn't give you front of line access are partially full of shit. It's true that the newer parks and rides, built after the "Americans with Disabilities Act" (ADA) requirements ruled the World, usually have fully accessible handicapped entrances via the regular queues. On those rides, you're waiting along with everyone else, and truth be told, the wait is often longer because you have to be seated in a special handicapped seat, and there are a limited amount of those on most rides.

However, at Magic Kingdom and EPCOT the large majority of the rides were built pre-ADA and thus the queues are too narrow or winding to fit wheelchairs. As a result, you usually get to skip the lines altogether and are ushered through a back entrance, effectively giving you front-of-line privileges. How well this works sometimes varies depending on how many other handicapped people are doing the same thing; sometimes the wheelchairs seem to be lined up further back than the real queue. But more often than not you go in through the exit of the ride, hop in one of the cars, and you're off; no waiting at all!

You don't even have to be in a wheelchair to gain access to the handicapped entrances! If you go to Customer Service at any of the parks you can receive a Guest Assistance Card (aka a GAC), which you show to the ride attendants for redirection to handicapped queues. If you're not actually in a wheelchair, though, you might not get any special treatment unless you have some invisible impairment. Obviously it's pretty easy to fake this, and a lot of people do just that, saying their kid has autism and can't wait in long lines, or they have MS and can't stand for extended periods of time, etc. Disney isn't legally allowed to request verification of this due to the ADA, so they just have to take people on their word.

It's more than a bit scummy to pretend to be disabled just to take advantage of FOL handicapped entrances, but if you are legitimately impaired, even temporarily, you should at least know that WDW is for the most part very wheelchair-friendly. If you do visit in a wheelchair it's best to bring your own, because their rentals are extremely expensive ($12/ day as of this writing). Alternately, the Utilidors entrance by Cinderella's

Castle always seems to have a stockpile of wheelchairs free for the taking.

I've also found that near the end of the day at the parks people will abandon their wheelchairs, apparently too lazy to turn them back in, since there's no deposit required. Although you aren't supposed to take wheelchairs out of the parks, you can take one of these abandoned wheelchairs and then either tell the people at the gate that you rented it at your resort, or that you need it to get back to your bus/boat/monorail. If you keep doing this you can essentially get a free wheelchair rental for the duration of your stay, which equates to a free front-of-line pass for quite a few rides.

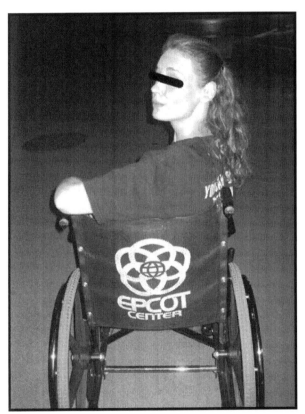

Hot girl in stolen wheelchair FTW!

So, without further adieu, here's a detailed list of rides that either have great Front-of-Line access for disabled guests, or really poor access that actually makes the wait longer than the normal line. If an attraction isn't mentioned that means that you go down the queue normally with everyone else.

All Parks:

- ❤ If you have a handicapped tag you get to park in the handicapped lots, which are right up front with the AAA lot!

Magic Kingdom:

- ❤ Jungle Cruise – You load in at the exit, boarding the boat before it moves to the regular queue. This equates to front-of-line access and usually zero wait time.
- ❤ Splash Mountain – Wheelchairs take a separate entrance which end at the exit ramp. Then you have to fight against oncoming traffic exiting from the ride, which is particularly risky around the blind corners. But you do get FOL access with no wait.
- ❤ Walt Disney World Railroad – Has a separate handicapped entrance for the front car of the train, which is extra-wide to accommodate wheelchairs. But since there is only this one seating area, if there are more than a few wheelchairs in line you'll probably end up waiting longer than the normal line. Either way, there's little advantage here.
- ❤ Thunder Mountain – Entrance through the exit queue = FOL! However, Thunder Mountain is extremely jarring and bumpy, so if you're with someone who is in a wheelchair because of back problems I don't recommend bringing them on the ride.
- ❤ The Haunted Mansion – We've been through two separate wheelchair entrances here. Both split off before the main queue, by the carriage. One time we were led by a CM part-way into the exit and then through a "Cast Members Only" door on the left that opened straight into the loading area. The other two times we were led all the way through the exit queue to the unloading area and boarded there. Both ways are FOL, no-wait, although the downside is that you skip the "stretching room", which is a bummer.
- ❤ Snow White's Scary Adventure – Entrance through the exit, straight onto the ride, bypassing the queue entirely. Awesome.

- Peter Pan's Flight – Same as "Snow White". This is a major timesaver.
- It's a Small World – You enter through the exit queue, but only specific boats are wheelchair accessible, and even with a few people in front of you the wait times are significant. Seems like it's about even with the normal queue.
- Space Mountain – Access is via the FastPass entrance. So this ends up being FOL, which kicks ass. Same bumpy/jerky warning as with Thunder Mountain, though.
- Buzz Lightyear's Space Ranger Spin – You do board at the unload area, but go through the queue with everyone else. You just get split off at the end. So no FOL.

Epcot:

- Spaceship Earth – Wheelchair access is via the exit. You sign in with a CM, then sit in a little waiting area, and eventually the CM leads you in through the exit. Depending on the crowds this might actually take longer than just going through the regular queue.
- Test Track – You go through the main queue but take a separate path after the theater that effectively bypasses the second half of the queue. Not exactly FOL, but if you have a FastPass it ends up being quite a timesaver.
- Living With the Land – There is a separate handicapped line that completely bypasses the normal line. Definitely FOL, and each boat can accommodate wheelchairs in the front row so no excessive waits like Small World.

Disney Hollywood Studios:

- The Great Movie Ride – You go through the first section of the queue, past all of the memorabilia, with everyone else. But once you get into the big room with the trailers showing, you get to bypass the long winding portion of the line. However, only one wheelchair can fit in each vehicle, so you might end up waiting a long time if there are a lot of wheelchairs ahead of you. This one is a toss-up depending on the crowds.

- Toy Story Midway Mania – This handicapped queue completely sucks! You go through the queue with everyone else but split off after picking up your 3D glasses. You're routed to a waiting area where you wait FOREVER because they have to re-route a ride vehicle to a side track. It seems like they only route every 200th car, which might be an exaggeration, but if there are three or for wheelchairs in front of you it can literally take an hour to get on the ride. If you can go through the regular queue on this one definitely do it!

Animal Kingdom:

- Dinosaur – This is setup a lot like Test Track. Wheelchairs go through the main queue, around the big dinosaur fossil, and into the theater. After the theater you take an elevator down to the vehicles, completely bypassing the regular winding line. Quite a timesaver!
- Kilimanjaro Safari – This is another horrible handicapped queue. You go along the regular line up to the point where it turns and starts doing switchbacks in front of the loading dock. You're redirected to a separate loading dock, where wheelchair-accessible busses are diverted. However, there are obviously very few of these special busses, and it can easily take 10x longer than the normal wait time if there are a bunch of other wheelchairs in front of you. Even if you're the only one there chances are your wait time will be longer than the normal queue. Lame.

Taking the Resort Monorail:

At the beginning and end of the day at Magic Kingdom the lines for the monorail and ferry between the Main Gate and The Ticket and Transportation Center are absolutely insane. You can literally wait an hour to get to the park or back to your car.

However, there is an alternate, although circuitous route to and from the Ticket and Transportation Center via the Resort Monorail. It takes a little longer since it stops at the resorts (The Polynesian and Grand Floridian on the way to the gates, and The Contemporary on the way back to the TTC), but you rarely have to wait for more than one monorail. I've never had them check that I was a Monorail Resort guest, although I have heard that during the busiest seasons they sometimes check for your room key.

The Resort Line Monorail pulling into The Contemporary

Usually at the end of the night after the fireworks even the Resort Monorail line is insane because everyone is flocking at once to get back to their hotel. And if it is the busy season and they are checking room keys, you're not getting on anyway. There is a way to get around both of these issues, however: take a relaxing and scenic five minute walk over to The Contemporary and board the monorail there! When you exit the gates of The Magic Kingdom simply go to the left and follow the well-marked trail of red bricks that leads past the busses (where a bunch of suckers are waiting for hours, probably), across a road, and around the resort's parking lot. Go into the hotel, up to the fifth floor, and hop on the monorail, no questions asked (why would you be getting on the monorail at the resort unless you were a guest there?). Nobody at The Contemporary will be going to either the TTC (because for normal guests there it makes no sense) or to MK (because it's closed), so the stop will be nearly empty.

Trail from MK to The Contemporary

SCAMS

FastPass Scams:

Wow, there are a ton of FastPass scams out there!
First up is the most obvious, namely counterfeiting. Sure, you can

counterfeit FastPasses; it's not like they're embedded with holograms or even barcodes. Supposedly counterfeiting was a big problem at first, and Cast Members were instructed to feel the edges of the ticket to make sure there were perforations in the proper places (the top and bottom). Apparently a lot of people were printing them out on cardstock at home and using a paper cutter to cut them out of bigger sheets, not realizing that actual FastPasses are distributed from a perforated roll. The obvious solution here is to use perforated cardstock (the kind used for business cards) or even better, rolls used for garment labels, which can be ordered online from a myriad of distributors. In order for this to be effective with the business card-type cardstock you'd buy from Staples, you'd still need to use a paper cutter to get clean edges on the sides, while retaining the perforation on the top and bottom.

Frankly, going through all of this time and effort to counterfeit FastPasses isn't worth it, unless you plan on selling them to suckers on eBay (which from the look of recent auction listings happens on a regular basis).

The better scams are the simpler and more clever ones. For example, there's the infamous "button" on the back of the FastPass machines: when you press it, a FastPass magically spits out! This only works if the CM on duty left the button unlocked, which in the past seemed to be done almost by default. Unfortunately too many people were using this scam and the CMs got wise to it and started locking all of the machines in a FP queue except for maybe one. So for this to work you'd possibly have to press the button on the back of each machine before you found the one that was unlocked, by which point the on-duty CM would have likely realized something was up. And the rumor mill now says that anyone caught pressing this button will be immediately escorted from the park. So probably not worth it.

However, you can still use this button trick to your advantage by getting the CM to press it for you! If you carry around an old, expired park ticket, when you insert it into the FP machine it'll spit back out without giving you a FP. These magnetic-strip tickets are easily demagnetized, and the CMs are too frazzled at busy times of the day to troubleshoot why your ticket won't work properly. So 99% of the time they'll just push the button for you! Score, free extra FastPass!

Another scam also preys on the volume of people the CMs have to deal with in regards to the FP systems. My friend Keith thought this up:

"I was there for a week one time and hadn't used a few of my prior days' FastPasses, and I was still carrying them around in my wallet. I went to Toy Story Mania and got my FP as usual, and then had to come back 45 minutes later. So I just shoved them into my wallet along with the ones from the previous day.

"Well, I showed the first CM the correct FastPass for TSM, and again, shoved it back into my wallet, thinking that was the end of it. But then the second CM later on in the queue wanted to actually collect the ticket, so I pulled it out of my wallet and gave it to her. She didn't even look at it, just took it from me, and we walked onto the ride.

"It was only when I got back to the resort and started dumping receipts out of my wallet that I realized I'd given her a FP from the previous day, and that the TSM one was still in my wallet!

"The possibilities for scamming seemed pretty vast once I realized that the second CM, the one who actually takes the tickets from you, doesn't check them. It's only the first CM at the beginning of the queue who checks them. So in theory you could collect a bunch of FPs from rides with no lines, and only one for a high-volume ride, and reuse the high-volume one to get on that really popular ride over and over throughout the day.

"I tried this out by getting a FP early on for Space Mountain. Before I rode Space Mountain each time I'd get a FP for Mickey's Philharmagic. I ended up keeping the 10AM Space Mountain FP I got and re-using that all day long, getting another FP from Mickey's Philharmagic each time I wanted to ride Space Mountain. By the middle of the day the Space Mountain FPs were totally gone, but I was able to keep going on it because I kept using the same 10AM pass over and over.

"Or you could even use the low-volume ones the next day, as I did by mistake. Assuming you're only going on low-volume rides you can collect upwards of 7-8 FPs throughout the day and use them all the following day after getting a single FP at the ride you want to go on over and over!"

I've also seen people selling FastPasses for Toy Story Mania later in the afternoon, when all of the FPs are gone for the day. People are standing there scalping them for $10 each, assumably already having gone on the ride a few times earlier in the day, and guests are flocking to buy them! If you have a family of 5 and can sell your FPs for $10 each you've almost paid for a park ticket. The passes do say "non-transferable" on them so technically this is illegal, but probably such a minor offense that the CMs won't enforce it.

Refillable Mugs:

This one is hilarious because it seems to piss so many people off. They get banned from message boards for being frothing-at-the-mouth batshit mad that other people are abusing the system to get free soda. Oh, the horror!

It's so simple it's hard to even call it a scam. The resorts all have mugs for sale at an inflated price that can be refilled as often as you want for the length of your stay. Guests will save their mugs and bring them back on their next trip so they can continue to get free refills without paying for another mug. There are accounts of people using 7+ year old mugs that are all worn down and disgusting, instead of simply paying another $12.50 for a new one! On top of that, a quick eBay search reveals that you can even buy someone else's used, scratched, dirty refillable mug for a fraction of the original cost, or sell yours after a few years and make back a portion of your original "investment".

As of this writing Disney doesn't crack down on this scam at all, although recent reports suggest that soon chips might be implanted in the cups, and they'll have to be scanned at the soda fountains before any soda will dispense. If the info on the chip doesn't match the date of your stay, no soda for you! However, it seems as if the cost of implementation of this system vs. the savings from cracking down on soda scammers would not balance out, so I think this is a rumor that won't ever come to fruition, and people will continue to use the same refillable mug for decades to come.

Pin Trading Scams:

Pin trading has got to be the stupidest hobby ever. They're too small to be very enjoyable from an artistic perspective, they serve no functional purpose, and they're insanely overpriced. However, the biggest reason for the extreme hate I feel for these pins is that they clog up the auction listings on eBay. If I do a search for Epcot, for example, literally ¾ of the listings will be for pins. So I always have to add –pin –pins to the end of my searches to weed them out.

But that speaks to the popularity of the damn things. And anything popular will eventually become the subject of a scam! This one comes from Tricia, a sweet, innocent-looking Orlando resident with a heart of coal. Her scam isn't exactly clever, but it is funny because it shows the lengths people are willing to go through to acquire these stupid little pieces of plastic and metal.

"I go to the parks every weekend, and after seeing how crazy people go over pin trading I realized it was ripe for exploitation.

"So I did some research and found that 'Hidden Mickey' pins were both popular and somewhat rare. So I bought the cheapest, most generic set of pins I could find off of eBay, and then went around one day at Epcot and traded each of those pins with Cast Members for Hidden Mickey pins. At this point I'm out $12 and a day of my time.

"The next day I go back to Epcot, knowing that all of the Hidden Mickey pins are gone from the CMs lanyards. So people are getting desperate trying to complete their collection by the end of their trip, but aren't having any luck with the CMs. I, on the other hand, am displaying said pins prominently on my lanyard and proceed to stand near one of the many pin-selling carts or stores. One by one people come up to me, asking if they can trade for one of my Hidden Mickey pins. I pretend to look hard at their lanyard and then tell them that they don't have anything I want.

"'However,' I'll say, 'I would like some of those pins from the new such-and-such set. If you buy four of them for me I'll definitely trade those for this here Hidden Mickey pin you want so badly.'

"So they freak out and rush over and buy the pins, and I nonchalantly ask if I can have the receipt for my collection to show when and where I got specific pins. They always hand over the receipt, and I hand them the Hidden Mickey pin, and they're thrilled even through they've just spent at least $15 on a little piece of junk.

"And the punch line, of course, is that I immediately return the pins to the pin cart or store for cash, and then move onto the next store/cart and repeat the scam all over again. The following weekend I'll go to a different park and do the same thing. I can easily clear $300 a day with this scam!"

To add onto Tricia's story, a fairly recent development is that the Chinese factories that manufacture the pins are not destroying the original molds, but are instead illegally selling them to people who then create thousands of counterfeit "scrappers", i.e., cheap knock-offs of high-demand pins from those same molds.

If a scammer knows where to look they can get these scrappers for pennies each, and either use those to trade for legitimate pins which they can then sell on eBay, or use them for the above scam, essentially saving themselves the day of trading with CMs.

So far Disney doesn't seem to give a shit about these counterfeits, and to be honest, some of the copies are so good that I'm not sure how they'd even begin to crack down on them, aside from making CMs take a daylong course on spotting counterfeits, which would just be a ridiculous waste of time and money. Eventually they'll probably try to crack down on the Chinese factories, but I doubt they'll have much luck with that, unless they're legitimately willing to move their business to more reputable factories, which would drive up the cost of pins exponentially.

If you don't want to get scammed when you're pin trading, there's a great site that shows pictures of legit pins: http://www.pinpics.com. If you have a Smart Phone with you in the parks it's relatively easy to search the site for the pin you're about to receive in trade to see if it's a scrapper or not. Hopefully they'll come out with a mobile app soon....

BED BUGS AND OTHER CREEPY-CRAWLIES

Bed bugs are pretty nasty little creatures. They feast on your blood at night, leaving huge burning welts that take weeks to heal. And if they follow you home from vacation (usually stowing away in your luggage) it will cost thousands of dollars to get rid of them because the only surefire way to kill bed bugs (aside from DDT, which is illegal) is by roasting them at 128-degrees or higher for more than 30 minutes. Unfortunately bed bug infestations have been on the rise over the past decade in the United States both because of the DDT ban and because of an increase in international travel.

There are some precautions you can take to cut down on the chances of being infected by this menace. When you get to your room, don't immediately start unpacking everything and then jump in the bed for a nap! Leave your luggage right outside the door and have one person go into the room with a small flashlight (the LED ones on key chains work great). Lift up the corners of the mattress and use the flashlight to check the mattress seams and the box spring for little brown or red specs (i.e.,

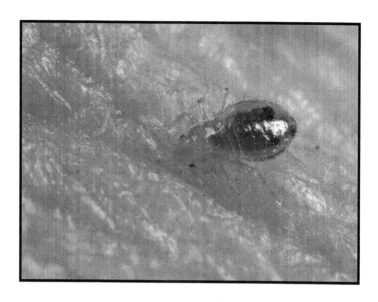

A bed bug doing what it does best. . . sucking your blood!

blood pooped out by bed bugs). You can also use a sticky-tape lint brush or the reverse side of a maxi-pad to wipe around the headboard, checking for the same brown specks or for actual bugs. If you find signs of the bugs, leave the room immediately and tell the front desk! If you don't see anything, then enjoy your bed bug free room.

If you do end up getting bitten while on vacation, it's going to be hard to tell if the bites are bed bugs. Unfortunately, Florida is home to a huge number of bloodsucking insects, so the bites could be fleas, fire ants, mosquitoes, or bed bugs. It could even be a simple heat rash. Luckily each type of bite/rash looks and feels noticeably different, so educate yourself beforehand so you'll know the difference; there are pictures all over Google Images comparing different types of bites. You'll also be able to narrow it down because ants and mosquitoes are fairly easy to spot, whereas fleas and bedbugs are smaller and better at hiding. Obviously, if you wake up and have the bites, as opposed to getting them while walking around the parks, chances are better that there are bed bugs in your room.

Finally, it's becoming more apparent that bed bugs are no longer just coming from beds. They've been found in high-class boutique clothing stores in NYC, in the cargo compartments of airplanes, and even in movie theater seats. So unless you plan on never leaving your house and never inviting anyone in to visit, you're going risk bed bug exposure and there's nothing you can do about it. So stop worrying and enjoy your vacation, dammit!

But people on Disney web forums refuse to take this advice and just LOVE to freak out about bed bugs. Like, totally apeshit panic attacks that threaten to ruin their vacation before they even leave. And the media isn't helping, with a different inflammatory story about the little bloodsuckers popping up in major publications every week or so. However, I contacted a number of people on Disboards who claimed to have been bitten by bed bugs at WDW, and it seems like a lot of these people are just trolls trying to stir up trouble. Only Yolanda, a single mother of two, had a story that sounded legit.

"We were staying at the Alligator Bayou section of Port Orleans Riverside," begins Yolanda. "I was in a double, my son was in the other double, and my daughter was in a trundle that pulled out from under my son's bed. The first morning all three of us woke up with painful red bites, which at first I thought were fire ant bites. But then I remembered reading about bed bugs a while ago on Disboards and realized I had totally forgotten to check the beds (won't make that mistake again!).

"Well, sure enough I found little brown flecks all over the back corners of the mattress, so I started freaking out a little bit! I frantically dragged both kids down to the Concierge Desk and told the gentleman behind the desk, Jerry, what happened. I was trying to be quiet so that the other guests wouldn't hear me, because I didn't want to start a panic, but when I showed Jerry the welts on my daughter's arms he screamed, "Oh no, bed bugs!" like a little girl! LOL!!!

"You would have thought we had Ebola the way they handled everything. First they bought us brand new outfits from the gift shop, made us take off our old clothes and seal them in plastic bags (always wear clean underwear, kids!), shower, and then put on the new clothes. Then they bagged up all of our luggage and anything else we had with us and took it away to be heat-treated, which they said might damage some polyester-based materials. We were also told that the mattresses would be thrown away and that our room would be treated and quarantined for at least a week.

"In the meantime we were moved to a bed bug-free 1-bedroom suite at Saratoga Springs, which was beautiful, and our entire stay was comp'd! Our clothes and luggage came back the next day, and only one of my sweaters was destroyed (it shrunk up, I guess from being washed in boiling water), which they also paid me for. All in all it wasn't the best experience, but Jerry and the rest of the staff really went out of their way to make sure our vacation wasn't ruined. I have no complaints about the whole thing, and would still stay at Port Orleans, except next time I'd check the bed before I slept in it!"

Personally, this doesn't sound so bad to me. Yolanda and her kids got free Disney clothes (i.e., free souvenirs!) and a free hotel stay. I'd be tempted to actually seek out a bed bug or two, let them bite me in a controlled environment, kill them, bring them to the front desk in a plastic baggie, tell them I found the bugs in my room, and then reap the rewards. A few bug bites for a cheap vacation?! Sign me up!

TIP: If you're really paranoid and are interested in exactly which rooms at which resorts have recently had bed bug infestations, visit http://bedbugregistry.com/hotel/FL/Orlando/Walt-Disney-World-Resort for up-to-date first-hand reports.

However, it should be stated that Central Florida is home to a literal swarm of wildlife much more dangerous than bedbugs, most of which can be found on WDW property. For example:

- *Alligators.* Where there's water in Florida, there are alligators. They're in Bay Lake, they're on the golf courses, they've even been known to roam around resorts and one was even found in Splash Mountain! No shit: http://www.youtube.com/watch?v=jiPSIgUx2Ls. They can move surprisingly fast, and can easily take a limb off in one bite, but to be honest they're usually just sitting around in the sun acting all fat and lazy. When Disney gets a report of an alligator on property they "relocate" it somewhere else (no idea what this actually means), but keep your eyes peeled on the waterways and you're pretty much guaranteed to see at least one gator on your vacation.

- *Water Moccasins and other Snakes.* Again, if you're near swampland in Florida, there are going to be snakes, and more than likely some of those will be water moccasins (also known as cottonmouths). These are thick brown snakes whose bites are quite poisonous. Furthermore, they're fairly aggressive buggers and unlike most

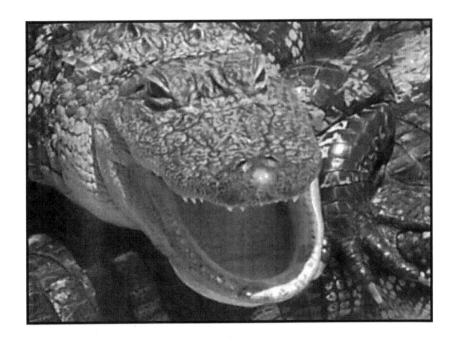

This alligator WILL EAT YOUR FACE!

If you see a snake in this pose, RUN THE FUCK AWAY!

wildlife will stand their ground or even approach intruders. While their bite won't kill a healthy adult, it will destroy a limb, and could certainly kill a child. There are a ton of other snakes in Florida that are perfectly harmless (and even cute at times) but if you can't tell the difference between a corn snake and a water moccasin then it's best just to run screaming from any slithering reptiles you encounter.

And just to further stoke the paranoia of those with snake phobias, snakes have been found INSIDE on-site hotel rooms! If you are deathly afraid of snakes, you absolutely should request NOT to have a ground floor room! They can get in under the sliding glass doors on ground level rooms and have been known to hide in the drapes or even in the beds. Again, I am not shitting you, there's a 33-page thread with pictures at Disboards: http://www.disboards. com/showthread.php?t=2116495

- ❦ *Fire Ants.* These aren't like ants in other parts of the US that just walk around and eat your food and annoy you. No, these giant red fuckers with huge venom sacks in their asses will get in your shoes, under your pants, in your underwear, in your hair, in your fucking ears and bite the fuck out of all of your most sensitive parts, leaving monstrous burning welts in their path. Enough of these bites can kill and infant or old person. These asshole ants are bad news! They build massive anthills in the dirt, so if you see a big cone-looking dirt pile, DON'T KICK IT OVER unless you want swarms of stinging red ants everywhere! Of course, as a kid, it was great fun to do just this and watch the ants go apeshit, or even better, to pour gas all over the anthill and light it on fire. These ants will show you no mercy, and they deserve none in return!

- ❦ *Cockroaches.* Living in Tampa for the first 18 years of my life, I assumed that cockroaches all over the US looked like the ones in Florida. Turns out, no, the ones in Florida are monster-sized versions of the tiny little things they have all over the rest of the country, so it's always entertaining when a non-native first sees one of these massively disgusting bugs and freaks out. Orlando roaches are huge, most clocking in at a 2" long or more, they fly, they make weird noises, and they are literally everywhere that food can be found. Yes, you will see them scurry across the floor at Disney restaurants, and yes, you might find them in your resort room. The

The bites of fire ants are among the most painful of any insect

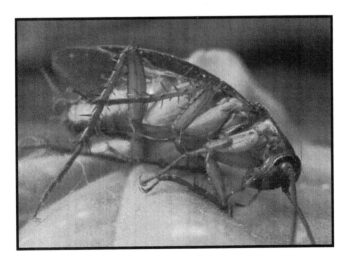

I promise, they have been walking in your food

worst thing is that if you see one, there are probably dozens more hidden away, just waiting for the lights to go down so they can swarm. In the worst infestations, you can go into a kitchen, turn on the light, and the countertop will be pure black, completely covered with roaches, who will then scatter into the walls in a matter of seconds. They carry diseases, they're hard to kill, and when you step on them green goo spills out. There is not much to love about cockroaches, as opposed to....

☙ *Love Bugs.* These black and orange flying bugs are literally a bunch of little fuckers. Twice a year for about a month they swarm over Florida, covering every brightly colored surface, getting clogged in radiators and smashed on windshields, and landing on your hair, in your eyes, in your mouth, etc. Which would be gross enough except that what first appears to be one long bug is actually two bugs joined together at the crotch, fucking until death! Have fun explaining that one to your kids!

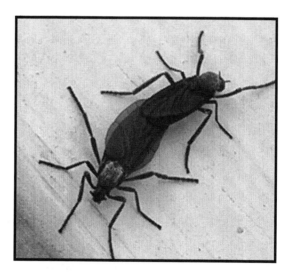

Good luck explaining this to your kids!

☙ *Brain Eating Amoebas.* Yes, it sounds like something out of a bad horror movie, that doesn't make it any less real. Naegleria fowleri is an amoeba that lives in the bottom of lakes and enters your body through the nose, where it hauls ass into the brain and proceeds to feast on your gray matter. Warmer temperatures allow it to replicate more, and it thrives in stagnant, shallow areas of a lake. Which is one of the main reasons why Disney no longer lets you swim in the beaches along Bay Lake, and is also why some think River Country was shut down. In 2007 six people died from the bacteria, and three of those deaths were in Orlando! If a single amoeba is inhaled into the nasal passages it can first cause flu-like symptoms, followed by hallucinations, and finally coma and death in as little as one day. So when the signs on the beach at The Polynesian tell you "No Swimming", they're not kidding around!

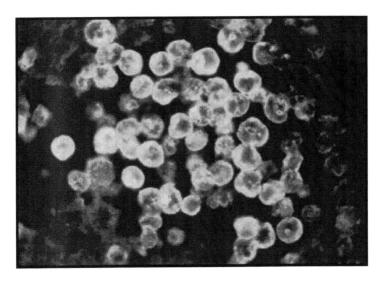

Naegleria fowleri look pretty, until they're eating your brain

4

Off-Limits Exploration

SNEAKING INTO THE UTILIDORS

It's your fourth or fifteenth trip to Walt Disney World. You love the place dearly, but by now you've gone on all of the rides many times over, explored all of the resorts, and eaten at all of the best restaurants. You've even traveled off-site to Universal and Sea World, and maybe even to The Orlando Love Loft. You've done it all, and the thought of going back and doing it all again seems a bit boring for an adventurous spirit such as yourself. But yet you're still drawn to Walt Disney World.... What to do?

This is the spot my friends and I found ourselves in back in the summer of 1995. Three guys who were born and raised in Clearwater, and who had all been to Walt Disney World more times than we could count. Hell, we used to go there on school field trips! Being total geeks, EPCOT was our favorite park, but we loved them all, and combined we'd probably made nearly 100 trips to *each park* in our lifetimes. It was a second home, and Walt Disney was our cool Uncle. But we were becoming adults, and wanted to rebel against the boredom of safety and false security Uncle Walt had provided us. We were too old to think that "It's a Small World" was fun, but not yet old enough to enjoy it on a nostalgic level. In short, if we were to keep going back to WDW, something had to give.

And it finally did give, for the better, the summer after our freshman year at college. I'd enrolled at a prestigious private university, purposefully getting out of driving distance from my family in Florida. Newmeyer, a pudgy nerd who'd never touched a girl (much to his dismay), had only reached Atlanta, where he was happily partaking in the social rewards of a veritable geekscapade at Georgia Tech. However, he'd started a disturbing shoplifting habit which at the time seemed harmless and funny, but which would eventually land him in jail. McGeorge, a lanky self-avowed anarchist and social outcast with bad skin, had stayed behind. He'd actually moved closer to The Mouse, going to school at UCF in Orlando. Out of the three of us, he'd changed the most, growing his hair out, drinking a lot, and nearly flunking out of school.

When we got back together in Tampa that summer, it was like no time had passed. We were still the best of friends, and were thrilled to have a few months to hang around each other again. But it seemed as if the outside world had changed: our parents were more annoying and demanding, our siblings were more childish, summer jobs were more tedious, and Walt

Disney World was... boring. I went a few times that summer with my family, and other than Space Mountain, Thunder Mountain, and the cheap thrill of seeing girls losing their bikini tops on the slides at Blizzard Beach, I was bored out of my skull. "RIP, Uncle Walt," I thought to myself.

The summer went by quickly, though. I had a job as a cart-pusher and bagger at Publix, which I promptly quit after three weeks because the idiot manager insisted cart-pushers wear dark slacks. Any guy who has ever worn dark slacks outside in the humid Florida summer heat knows that you sweat like a pig, and the sweat drips down your back, onto your pants, and quickly forms white rings of dried salt below the band of the pants. Not to mention the soaked armpits on the knit polo shirts we had to wear. Judicious application of Right Guard stopped the stench but still couldn't stop the actual sweat from soaking your entire body. Sweating like this and going back inside to bag groceries made me look and feel disgusting, and I felt awful touching people's groceries and trying to be polite when I was desperately in need of an hour-long shower.

So much to my mother's dismay I quit the grocery store job and started a band with Newmeyer and McGeorge. We played a nonsensical mix of Gershwin, The Beatles, Zappa, and death metal. I was on guitar and vocals, Newmeyer on bass, and McGeorge on drums and keyboards. We played the local coffee shop on the weekends and I made more money each weekend than I'd been making each week at Publix. "Fuck Publix, and fuck my mom for making me get such a bullshit job!" I proclaimed triumphantly. I was in full-on adolescent asshole mode. But things were going great with the band, and we'd each saved up enough money for an end-of-summer trip.

"I don't want to go to Daytona!" yelled Newmeyer.

"Why not, you dick?" I shouted back.

"Will you two shut the fuck up?" screamed McGeorge, desperately concentrating on trying to download a single pornographic picture from a BBS over a state of the art 14.4K baud modem.

"I'm fat, and everyone will be walking around in bathing suits," seethed Newmeyer, completely ignoring McGeorge. "I'm not taking my shirt off!"

I sighed. "Sweet Christ. Okay, fine. So no beaches? It's Florida, dumbass! Where are we going to go where there's not a beach?"

"Let's go to Disney," replied McGeorge, not looking up from his computer. "Fuck! The connection got reset! MOM!!!" He jumped up, opened his door, and started screaming into the hallway, beet red. "DID YOU JUST PICK UP THE PHONE?! I TOLD YOU TO ASK ME BEFORE USING THE PHONE!" He slammed the door. "We're going to Disney! Now stop your bitching and whining and help me download this porn!"

Newmeyer and I looked at each other and shrugged.

"Really, Disney?" I asked, incredulously. "That sounds a bit boring, McGeorge."

"No, wait..." started Newmeyer, staring up at the ceiling. "It's perfect! We can stay at a fleabag motel, get our Florida discount on the tickets, and McGeorge can hook us up with a shit ton of booze through his UCF connections."

"Yeah," said McGeorge, not paying any attention to us. "I'm awesome. Porn."

"I've already been there like eighty times this summer with my mom and my sister," I said, getting a bit desperate. "It was boring! McGeorge!" I yelled, breaking him out his modem-noise induced stupor. "Can you seriously get us booze?"

"Yes, yes, fine," he wearily replied. Suddenly he jolted back to reality. "Wait, I just remembered something. Check this shit out."

He cancelled his porn download, and Newmeyer and I gasped. "This must be awesome," I thought.

After ten minutes of BBS searches, McGeorge connected to a server and downloaded an ASCII map (i.e., a map drawn with text characters, thus taking up significantly less bandwidth than an actual line-based image) of The Utilidors, the secret network of tunnels underneath The Magic Kingdom, restricted to Cast Members only. And so it began....

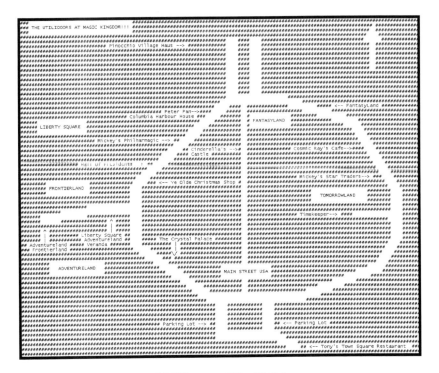

ASCII map of The Utilidors

We memorized the map, borrowed a video camera from McGeorge's uncle, and headed up to Kissimmee. McGeorge actually cut his hair and shaved in anticipation of the trip to The Utilidors, knowing that his faux-hippie appearance was totally contrary to "The Disney Look" and would immediately get us singled out from the rest of the Cast Members down there. Newmeyer and I also showed up that morning clean shaven and with our hair more closely cropped than usual.

When we got to the main gate we backtracked until we found the closest motel we could afford, dropped off our suitcases, loaded up our backpacks, and headed out to The Magic Kingdom.

Pulling up to the far right booth of the Main Parking Gate, McGeorge started in on a scam we'd cooked up. "Uh, we're, uh, here to meet a friend at The Contemporary," stuttered McGeorge.

The lady at the booth seemed unconvinced. "Name?" she demanded.

"Uh…" McGeorge looked at me. I shrugged. "Uh… Frank… Sinatra?"

"Seriously?" asked the wrinkled booth operator.

"Yeah," piped up Newmeyer from the backseat. "Friend of the family! Didn't you know he was staying at The Contemporary this weekend?"

She screamed across to the booth to her left. "Bill! Is Frank Sinatra staying at The Contemporary this weekend?"

"I dunno?" slurred Bill. "Maybe? Yeah, maybe." He furtively swigged from a flask. "Sinatra!"

We all cheered. Wrinkly Booth Operator pushed a button and the gate lifted. "You boys better be telling the truth!" she exclaimed as we drove off, veering to the left, away from The Contemporary and heading directly for The Magic Kingdom's parking lot.

"Fuck paying for parking!" I yelled, and we all cheered. This was going to be an awesome trip.

After taking the tram from the lot to the Ticket and Transportation Center, McGeorge and Newmeyer bought their tickets, bitching about the price, but still happy that they'd received a sizeable discount with their Florida IDs. I had a "Four Season Salute" pass, courtesy of my mom.

"Pretty cool that your mom got that for you," said McGeorge as he shelled out his hard-earned band cash for a ticket.

"Yeah…. It was pretty cool, I guess." I replied. For the first time that summer I actually had something nice to say about my mother.

We took the Resort Monorail from the Ticket and Transportation Center to the park. I liked seeing The Polynesian and Grand Floridian on the way in, and the line was always significantly shorter for the Resort Monorail than it was for either the ferry or the direct-to-gate monorail. That was the day we found the "hidden dick" on the monorail, a distinctly ball and cock shaped moulding attached to the door hinges. Many obscene pictures would be taken over the years next to these mouldings….

It's hard to get off the monorail, go through the gates at The Magic Kingdom, and not feel a sense of nostalgia. Even if you've never lived in a small town that has a "Main Street", there is something in the American cultural subconscious that Walt Disney tapped into here. Some sort of zeitgeist that we can all relate to on an almost genetic level. Walking through the train station tunnel and seeing Main Street, and catching a glimpse of the castle on the horizon produces a visceral reaction in even the most jaded citizens. And Newmeyer, McGeorge, and I were about as jaded as you could be at that point. Yet we paused at City Hall, looked at

Cinderella's Castle, and turned to each other, smiling at the anticipation of a whole new sort of Disney adventure.

"Let's do this!" I shouted, and we charged towards the castle, knowing exactly what our first ride would be. Not Space Mountain, or Thunder Mountain, or Mr. Toad's Wild Ride. No, we were headed straight for The Utilidor entrance immediately northwest of the castle.

We sprinted through the rose garden leading up to the castle, taking in the sounds and smells of our surroundings. Exhilarated, running full speed, we quickly reached the location detailed in our ASCII map.

But we saw... nothing. No heavily barricaded door, no "Keep Out" sign, no semi-obvious security cameras, no plain-clothed Disney cops, no off-limits entrance whatsoever. Dismayed, we parted shrubbery, looked under the bridges for secret ladders, and kicked at the pavement for trap doors.

"Fuck!" I yelled, causing a lady nearby to glare at me and cup her hands over her daughter's ears. "Give me a break, lady!" I shouted to her, and turned to McGeorge. "Your map sucks!" I was pissed. "I can't believe we came all the way here, spent money on a hotel, and then it turns out the damn map is a fake! We're all a bunch of idiots for believing some anonymous jackass on some stupid BBS!"

"Yeah, McGeorge, I'm never listening to your damn modem butt-buddies again!" shouted Newmeyer.

"Shove it, Newmeyer, my computer is smarter than you'll ever be!" spat a flustered McGeorge as he punched Newmeyer in the arm, hard. Newmeyer immediately put McGeorge into a headlock, and they both fell on the ground.

"Get off me, fatass!" screamed McGeorge, his voice raised an octave into an ear-piercing shriek, causing birds to scatter.

Disgusted, I turned and started walking away, not wanting to be there when the Disney Police showed up.

And then I saw it. Just beyond the simple and unobtrusive Sleeping Beauty fountain was a double door with two smooth black handles, completely inconspicuous in the shadows with its bland brown and slightly dirty turquoise paint, contrasted with the shimmering ornate gold trim on the nearby castle. No warning signs, no locks, no lights, nothing drawing attention to itself in the midst of a whole park which was having the exact opposite effect on the senses. A door specifically designed to not be noticed. Brilliant.

The Mythical Utilidors Entrace Next to Cinderella's Castle

"Guys!" I yelled under my breath. Newmeyer was on top of McGeorge, a long thread of phlegm hanging from his mouth, dangling above McGeorge's face. McGeorge screamed, and it was so loud I just about bolted then and there. "Assholes, the door is right in front of us!" I hissed.

Newmeyer sucked the spit back into his mouth, jolted around, and jumped off of McGeorge. "What, where?!"

I pointed to the door. Newmeyer gasped.

McGeorge got up with a frenzied grin, apparently forgetting he'd come within a second of having a puddle of snot dropped onto his face. "Fuck me, that's smart!" he laughed.

We all stood there, staring at the door. Breaking out of my stupor, I quickly realized that security would be arriving any second. "Guys, we need to get out of here, and fast."

"Down the rabbit hole?" asked Newmeyer apprehensively.

"That's what we came here for," responded McGeorge.

So I walked to the door, opened it, and stepped inside. Newmeyer and McGeorge followed right behind me, and the door closed silently behind us.

And what we saw was completely anticlimactic: an ugly fluorescent-light lit room with a large pile of wheelchairs and strollers in the corner, stacked two high, and a stairway whose handrails were covered with chipped paint. A cockroach scurried across the floor.

Currently there are strollers stored in the entry room

"Lame," I said.

"Blech," echoed McGeorge.

"Well, at least now we know where to go to get a free wheelchair," a chipper Newmeyer chimed in. "Seriously, I'm sure all the good stuff is down the stairs."

I nodded in agreement, and we started the trek down the two stories of stairs. We were almost at the bottom when I thought I heard a noise, freaked out, and ran back up both flights, two steps at a time. The guys followed, freaked out by my freak-out. We got back to the top room, trying to stifle our heavy breathing.

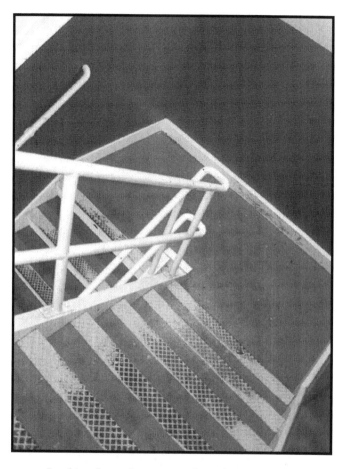

Looking down the stairway from the entry room

"What the fuck, Kinsey?" whispered an out of breath and out of shape Newmeyer.

"Ssshhh, shut up, I heard something."

We all listened intently. Not a sound.

"Goddammit, Kinsey!" sighed an exasperated McGeorge. "Newmeyer's fat heart can't handle this shit!"

I laughed, Newmeyer scowled, and we started walking down the steps again.

At the bottom was a sign warning about asbestos. "Weird," I said, as the other guys nodded in agreement.

We opened the door and found ourselves in an empty hallway. Another door was on the left, and the right seemed to open out into a tunnel... The Utilidors! We turned right, walked down to the tunnel and stopped short. Passing by us were Goofy, without his head on, his flamboyantly gay "handler" who was talking to him "in character", and Snow White, who Goofy was heavily flirting with.

"Now Goofy," intoned the handler with a high-pitched lisp, "I don't want to hear any of that sort of talk!"

Goofy grabbed Snow White's ass as well as he could with his huge padded hand. She gasped and punched him in the nuts. He laughed, obviously protected by the costume's padding, and tried to grope her left breast. She sighed and kissed him.

The handler continued to blabber on. "Goofy, that sort of behavior simply isn't appropriate! Mickey is going to punish you when he gets home!"

They walked past the tunnel entrance, and we glued ourselves to the wall as they went by, going completely unnoticed.

"What... the... fuck?!" I murmured. It was like some crazy alternate reality down here, like we really had gone down Alice's rabbit hole.

"Let's follow them!" said an overly excited McGeorge. "Snow White is hot!"

Seemed like a reasonable plan. We certainly had no idea where we were going, so why not follow people who did? We stepped out into the tunnel... and nearly got run over by a battery-powered golf cart silently barreling down the middle of the walkway.

"Watch where you're going assholes!" yelled the driver.

Shaken but undeterred, we continued onwards, following Goofy and his two admirers. Journey's "Separate Ways" played through the speakers overhead, followed by Bryan Adams' "Summer of 69". No Disney music down here, assumably to offer a respite to the Cast Members from the constant barrage of it in the park overhead. Although whether Bryan Adams was a sanity-saving alternative to the Sherman Brothers was certainly debatable.

The Utilidors under Fantasyland

A wide variety of Cast Members passed us, costumed, half-costumed, or in street clothes, completely oblivious to our presence. It was like we were invisible. So we kept walking, even when our Goofy-led escorts turned off and went up a random stairway. The one-foot wide stripe painted along the wall of the tunnel eventually changed color, and after stopping to stare slack-jawed at a full-color version of our ASCII map on the wall, we ascertained that this meant we were entering a different "land", in this case going from Fantasyland to Tomorrowland.

"Hey, I just realized something," I said, turning to the guys. "We had a hell of a time finding this one entrance. It'd be a lot easier to find them by coming out of them rather than trying to track them down from the outside."

"Yeah, good idea!" exclaimed McGeorge.

"I agree," said Newmeyer. "That'll save a ton of time. Let's go up the next stairway we see."

So we did, and on the way up a group of Cast Members going down the stairs squeezed past us. We nodded to them and continued on, still stunned that nobody seemed to care that we were down there. At the top of the stairs we were greeted with a scattered mess of clothing racks, filled with t-shirts ticketed with ridiculously marked-up price tags. Boxes piled high along the walls were filled with stuffed animal versions of the characters. The room easily contained $10,000 worth of merchandise, and there was nothing stopping us from grabbing a handful. But just then a female security guard turned the corner. We froze, not knowing whether to run and hide or stand our ground. I made the decision for us.

"Excuse me, M'am," I started. "It's our first week here, and we're a bit lost. Just trying to get out to Tomorrowland?"

She turned and pointed the direction she'd just come from. "Right down that hall," she said cheerfully.

"Thanks!" we all said at once, as she continued down the stairway we'd just come up.

We breathed a sigh of relief and walked down the hallway she'd pointed to, coming to a set of double doors. We opened them and were blasted with blindingly bright light. Stepping outside, as our eyes adjusted to the daylight we turned back to see a pair of white doors, framed in silver and surrounded by a blue wall. As before, nothing there drawing attention to itself; no signs, no fancy ornamentation. Just plain white doors.

The Utilidor entrance in Tomorrowland

"Awesome," sighed McGeorge.

"I just about shit my pants when that security guard came by," said Newmeyer.

"She didn't care! Nobody cared!" I laughed.

We spent the rest of the day down in The Utilidors, going up every stairway, finding every entrance into the park above. Each time upon turning to see where we'd exited, we were greeted with a nondescript doorway, leading from the ultra-clean faux reality of The Magic Kingdom into a dirty, dingy, ill-kept hallway leading to a stairway. The transition was always jarring.

Random CM not caring we're down there

We found the employee bank, the costume rental window, multiple break rooms, and a cafeteria. The best find of the day was a doorway that led to an alcove under the seating in The Hall of Presidents, and it was almost like being under the bleachers in a stadium. We amused ourselves for a while listening for the audience to filter in and then beating on the underside of the seats during the show, laughing as people screamed about the ghosts of dead presidents.

Hall of Presidents Utilidor entrance

Eventually the day drew to a close. Exhausted from endless trips up and down two flights of stairs, we stumbled down Main Street, and drove back to our hotel. We spent the evening dangling our feet over the third floor walkway outside of our room, drinking beer, smoking hand-rolled cigarettes, and excitedly going over the details of the day.

Walt Disney World had become fun again.

In the years since I've continued to visit The Utilidors, never once encountering any sort of resistance. In fact, even post 9/11, I'm still shocked by how lax security is down there. Some highlights:

- Went back down with McGeorge and videotaped the entire walk from Frontierland to Tomorrowland with the videocamera held by my side. It was shaky, but produced some great shots, including a Chip/Dale head poking out of a dumpster and a semi-costumed

Cinderella making out with (and getting felt up by) a random CM against a wall. Broadcast this video on the student TV station at my prestigious Ivy League university at least 200 times, and never received any feedback. Apparently I was the only Disney Geek at school.

❦ As a summer camp counselor I brought down two separate groups of 15 teenagers as part of a fake "tour group". Acted like a tour guide, walking backwards the whole time and pointing out specific landmarks to the gawking kids.

❦ On a recent trip with my mom, who is admittedly not a risk-taker, I got fed up by the blockades setup for the daily parade. We had Fast-Passes and needed to get from Frontierland to Fantasyland to ride Peter Pan. So I dragged her, my wife, and my little brother down the Hall of Presidents entrance, through The Utilidors, and back up to the castle door. I think it was probably the most "dangerous" thing she'd done in 30 years, and she's still telling her friends how cool it was. When she asked how I knew how to get down there, I told her the story above and her response was, "Well, at least you weren't into drugs and sex like everyone else your age." Sigh.

❦ Google Earth has made finding the Utilidor entrances from the comfort of your own home fun and safe. It's like a scavenger hunt! For example, load up Google Earth and type in coordinates Lat 28°25'10.69"N, Long 81°34'53.32"W, with an eye altitude of 30m (go to the Ground-Level view of around 100ft). You'll see a lovely 3D rendering of our first and most beloved Utilidor entrance, WITH THE FUCKING DOOR OPENED!!!

BACKSTAGE AT EPCOT

While there is no complex Utilidor system at Epcot (just a very small set of rooms under Spaceship Earth) there is an extensive backstage area that circles the entire park, along with some very interesting sights to be seen. If you want to see some of them legitimately you can take the "UnDISCOVERed Future World" tour, which, for fans of the park who probably already know most trivia, is 75% fluff, 25% cool stuff. However, it's just as easy to get backstage yourself and walk around!

Probably the easiest access is from The Land. There are two ways to get backstage from this pavilion: you can either go out the large set of doors on the bottom floor to the left of Soarin', just past the bathrooms. If you sit there waiting for your significant other to finish taking a massive dump chances are you'll see at least a few CMs exiting through these doors. The other way to get backstage from The Land is to hang a sharp right immediately after getting off of Soarin', instead of walking down the exit hallway with everyone else. There's a single door that leads outside.

Path from Soarin to Omnimover maintenance area and back out to Imagination

Both of these exits will place you in the back of The Land, and you can travel east to get behind the Imagination Pavilion. On the tour they show you an area in the back of Imagination, across from the Canada Pavilion, where the 3D glasses are washed. But of more interest (and what is not elaborated on in the tour) is that next to this glass-washing station is the repair area for the Omnimovers used in the ride. If you've ever wanted to see up close the underside of an Omnimover you can duck underneath the raised track and take a gander. Spare parts and repair tools line the walls, and you can even walk back to the left to see where the track splits off from the main ride, designed so the disabled cars can be moved off the main ride track without having to pick them up with a crane or forklift.

Once you're done browsing this area you can exit back into Future World through a door that leads to the rear of Imagination, near the almost always empty restrooms on the right side of the pavilion.

Another relatively easy access point is via the Mission: Space queue. Apparently when they built this ride they expected a much larger crowd, because there is a huge abandoned stretch of queue on the side of the pavilion. The easiest way to get to it is to go up the ramp on the right side. This leads to a winding area, and just before the line snakes into the building there is an exit to the right that leads to a loading dock. Take the steps down and you'll find a dirt path that actually runs under the Test Track exterior track, and from there to a series of parking lots and roads that wind around the entire park. If you head south you'll find the Costuming and general CM building on your left. It's worth looking at, as there's no ID required to enter. Continue south past China and around the docks where they store the Illuminations globe, and you'll find yourself behind the "Africa" area, which was once supposed to house a Pavilion (and might still yet, if Disney execs ever get their asses in gear and throw some more cash at Epcot). The land is cleared, but there's nothing there except a dumping ground for old props and Food and Wine Festival booths. What's dumped back there seems to rotate (and rot) but right now the boneyard features various ride structures and is the rumored burying ground of some of the 20K Leagues subs!

My off-limits escapades are small-time compared to the exploits of other daring souls I've met via the wonders of The Interwebs. McGeorge's BBSs had transformed into "Al Gore's Internet", and suddenly like-minded souls started coming out with some crazy stories of WDW infiltrations that rivaled military operations. I've had the pleasure and honor of getting

Path from Mission: Space queue to CM Costuming building

to know two of these brave characters, and both agreed not only to let me interview them, but to also allow a few of their adventure photos to be published.

INTERVIEW WITH SHANE PEREZ

First up is Shane Perez, a good-looking, well-spoken Miami native now residing in NYC. Shane received a certain amount of notoriety after exploring an abandoned rocket silo which still contained one of the most powerful rockets ever made! Thrilling video of him rappelling down the side of the underground silo (and nearly getting stuck) was featured prominently in the 2007 documentary *Urban Explorers: Into the Darkness*. This movie, by Melody Gilbert, focuses on men and women who, often at great risk to their safety, explore abandoned industrial sites, an activity known as "Urban Exploring". The film examines their motivations for engaging in this high risk activity, and highlights the sense of wonder and beauty that these individuals feel from witnessing firsthand the crumbling and decaying architecture and technology of years past.

But Shane received even more attention beginning on Christmas Day, 2009 when he published a blog entry on his website, http://shaneperez. blogspot.com, featuring a detailed report of his trip to Discovery Island, Walt Disney World's long-abandoned nature park. Discovery Island, located in the heart of Bay Lake, was left to rot years ago when the opening of Animal Kingdom effectively rendered the previously well-maintained zoo obsolete. Instead of bulldozing the property, Disney simply decided to leave it as-is and let nature take its course, turning it into an overgrown urban ruin that was an irresistible destination for Shane and his fellow Urban Explorers.

The gorgeous pictures from Shane's evening on the island, along with his well-written travelogue immediately made it clear that he wasn't a bragging punk kid trespasser, but was in fact an intelligent, talented individual whose admittedly outrageous story couldn't be easily dismissed as hooliganism. The Orlando Sentinel eventually broke the story and soon it was being reported on by media outlets nationwide, making Shane's previously underground celebrity status a thing of the past. Message boards at Disney fan sites buzzed with debate about whether Shane's actions, although obviously illegal, were also immoral, or at the very least just really stupid. But Shane kept his cool, firing back non-inflammatory and well-reasoned responses to his detractors basically saying, "Hey, I'm not hurting anyone except maybe myself, and that's none of your business."

I caught up with Shane almost a year after his blog post was published, and he graciously agreed to answer my sometimes long-winded questions.

What's your "day job"? Obviously Urban Exploring doesn't pay cash dividends…. Or does it?

I do home theater installation and I also work as a freelance photographer for the NY Post.

Describe for me what you get out of Urban Exploring on an emotional, or for lack of a better word, "spiritual" level. In other words, what is it about UE that fills a need that isn't fulfilled by normal everyday life?

I don't really see it as an activity, it's more of a way of looking at the world. It's about satisfying curiosity about how things work and their history. It also encourages me to exercise my critical thinking skills and learn to take responsibility for my own actions. Normal everyday places are set up to be as safe and foolproof as possible. You can basically wander through life on autopilot and never have to worry about being hurt or killed, there's always going to be a handrail or safety measure in place to protect you from yourself. That is not so in the places that I visit and I feel like that encourages me to be a more capable and aware human being by gaining more understanding of my surroundings.

Is the danger a part of the appeal? Personally, I'd love to explore a lot of these places, but the thought of getting arrested, even more so than getting physically injured, serves as a fairly strong deterrent. If danger isn't part of the appeal, how do you reconcile the obvious risks with the less obvious rewards?

Danger is not a motivating factor. I'd be just as happy seeing these places if it were completely legal and I had permission. Danger is everywhere really, you can get hit by a bus crossing a street, or slip in the shower and drown in 2 inches of water just as easily as you could get hurt by walking around an abandoned building. People may see what I do as "dangerous" but if you look at the numbers of people dying from heart disease, I'd say that it's a lot more dangerous to sit at home and watch TV while eating junk food. I'm not a thief or vandal, so as far as arrest goes I don't worry about it too much besides trespassing tickets which are usually just a fine.

Do you find yourself needing to justify these activities to your friends/family/ coworkers? Do you come across a lot of people who just don't understand your rationale? If so, how does that impact your relationships? I imagine if this is something you're passionate about it would be hard to maintain a relationship with someone who didn't understand risking your life for that passion.

Not particularly. I'm an adult and I don't really feel the need to justify any of my actions to anyone other than myself. I've come across a couple people that don't understand why I choose to do these things, but for the most part people get why I do it and many times tell me stories of similar things they have done in the past, often in their childhood. I get way more people asking to come along or saying that they wish they could but are unable to because of the risks involved. I don't really think I would have much interest in having any sort of relationship with anyone that is so caught up with rules and regulations that they can't fathom why I might do this, so it's mostly irrelevant. My friends/family/lovers vary in their level of understanding/support/interest, but none are completely opposed to it or lack understanding of why it is appealing.

Is there any place that is "sacred ground" to you? Or is it all fair game for exploring?

There are plenty of places I won't go, it's all dependent on the risk/reward ratio. There are tons of things I would love to see, but are quite unlikely I ever will. I would love to see the inside of an active nuclear power plant, NASA facilities, and many other similarly high security locations but those sorts of places are virtually impossible to see without permission. I basically stay away from any place that is a guaranteed arrest or that I feel are beyond my physical capabilities.

So you were born and raised in Miami, FL. How often did you visit Walt Disney World when you lived in Florida? Was it a rare treat, or did you visit often enough for the novelty to wear off? Do you have fond memories of family experiences there, or was it more of an annoyance to have to keep going back?

I went a few times with my folks growing up, but we didn't go too much. It was fun at the time, although I didn't particularly enjoy standing around in lines all day and I was always curious about behind the scenes stuff.

What was your first Urban Exploring experience at Walt Disney World? How long had you been doing this before you tried it at WDW?

It was probably exploring the Utilidor system a few yeas ago, a few months before I did the swim to Discovery Island. I had been dating a girl that worked there in the past and she taught me some of the Disney jargon and explained some of the rules about employee conduct/appearance. I also looked at a few maps online of the system and had a rough idea of where entrances should be. I dressed and cut my hair to meet Disney regulations, bought a ticket to the park and headed for an entrance determined to get in. I failed at the first entrance because I ran into a group of executives (including Michael Eisner!) coming out from the Utilidors and I got spooked. I bailed on that entrance and eventually found my way down after talking to a cast member outside of a ride and convincing them I was a new employee that was a little lost. Once I was down I spent quite a bit of time looking around, seeing the costuming areas, locker rooms (including the unisex one connecting them), computers that run the rides, the waste disposal system, and even had lunch in the employee cafeteria. It was a pretty good time and I even managed to sneak a few photos from my pocket.

I'd probably been exploring for a good 5 years at that point, so I was pretty confident in my abilities to blend in and talk my way out of trouble.

So let's get into the Discovery Island exploration. Had you been there as a child? If not, how did you find out about it?

Nope, I never actually went there while it was open. I heard about it from some local Orlando explorers that had read about it.

It seems like there was a primary, aborted attempt to reach the island. Explain why that first attempt failed, and what drove you to take the time to plan a comeback instead of just giving up?

Well, it basically came down to bad intel. The locals that had scouted it out before we came up had told us that there was "infrequent" traffic on the lake and that it was only about 150ft to the island from the nearest land. We snuck an inflatable boat, pump, and 200ft of clothesline into the campground and planned on paddling across and then pulling the boat back to the other side using the clothesline so we could ferry multiple people across. When we got there it turned out it was more like 300ft to the island at least and there were 2 ferries that crossed directly in the water between us and the island every 5-10 minutes. It was pretty much impossible to do the way we had planned and it was far too cold to swim when we were there. I vowed to come back and figure out a way to do it in the future.

How much planning went into this second attempt? Was there a "mission statement" of sorts? In other words, did you know in advance what you wanted to accomplish, and how exactly you would go about accomplishing it? Was there a specific "money shot" you felt you needed to get, or was it more of a "this is how we'll get over there, and once we're there we'll see what happens" sort of thing?

There was a fair bit of planning in terms of getting to the island, but none really for once we got there. We had no idea what we would find when we got there, so we left that in the air. We bought waterproof bags and tested swimming an equivalent distance with them in a lake behind my friend's house in FL. We took towels, changes of clothes, snacks, water, and camera gear to explore. We planned on giving ourselves a few hours on the island and set a hard "turn around" time where we would start heading back regardless of if we'd seen the entire island or not.

Did you know about the gators and the "killer amoeba"[Naegleria fowleri, which gets into your brain via your nose and is almost always fatal] when you decided to swim across the lake?

Not really. We had talked about the possibility of gators, but we just figured that since it was a "Disney" lake they wouldn't allow there to be gators that could come up on shore and potentially hurt guests.

Describe to me what was going through your mind as you're swimming across Bay Lake in the middle of the night? This is the scariest part of the tale for most people, because it taps into some primordial fear about swimming in the dark, especially in the ocean or in a lake....

It was pretty intense but what was in the lake itself was the least of our worries. We were mostly concerned with getting caught by the occasional lake patrols and landing in a good spot on the island. Most of the swim was spent looking back towards fort wilderness and the area where we knew lake patrol docked their boats. We tried to swim as quietly and quickly as we could.

Path Shane swam from River Country to Discovery Island

Once you hit land, you basically had no idea what was there, right? I mean, there could be polar bears like in "Lost"! Were you jumping at every little noise? Was it stressful being there, or was the total abandonment and desolation peaceful in some way?

Yeah, we had absolutely no clue what we were going to run into. We were definitely tense pretty much the entire time we were there. We were most definitely NOT alone on that island, there must have been thousands of birds nesting on the island and they all made their presence known. There were a lot of crashes and movement going on in the woods around us and everything was incredibly overgrown. We also were trying to use as little lights as possible to avoid being seen from the land so we really had no idea what was in the woods around us. We did take some video footage while there, I'm sure at some point I'll get it digitized and share it on my site for people to be able to have a better idea of what it was like on that island.

WTF was with the snakes in the jars and Coke bottles?! Any theories about that?

Your guess is as good as mine. Maybe they were snakes that were found on the island that someone kept to try and identify?

And you had a run-in with vultures?!

Yeah, they were relatively young and hadn't grown feathers in. They were in a collapsed building and were not terribly happy to see us. They made a lot of hissing noises and charged at us a few times trying to scare us off. We took a few photos and a bit of video and left their little area.

You've explored many corporate ruins; how does Discovery Island compare to the rest of them, and what does leaving a theme park to rot instead of cleaning it up and/or bulldozing it say about Disney as a company?

Discovery Island is a pretty unique thing in that it is totally abandoned and is reverting to a natural state. Most of the other theme park related things I've seen are behind the scenes areas or are only temporarily closed. I don't think it really makes a lot of sense to bulldoze the island, from what I saw there weren't a ton of buildings to begin with, just a lot of wilderness. I think letting the island revert to nature is a pretty obvious choice if they don't have a viable business plan for revamping it.

Any official kick-back from Disney? I know you waited until the statute of limitations ran out to post about the story, but there was talk of them banning you from the parks for life....

I haven't heard anything from Disney in any official way, but I also haven't tried going to any of their parks. It wouldn't be the end of the world if I were banned from the parks for life. If anything, it would make for a good story to tell.

Your series of nudes are absolutely stunning. Have you done any WDW nudes?

Thank you, unfortunately I haven't had the chance to shoot any nudes at WDW. I'm not really sure Discovery Island would work for my series, but I'm open to the possibility if I found a location that was good enough for it.

What's next for you? Any upcoming Urban Exploration projects on the horizons that you can talk about?

I've got a few things in the works, but I really don't like talking about that sort of stuff before I do it for obvious reasons. This year I've also been focusing more on having some gallery shows and establishing a bit of a presence in the art world.

Thanks, Shane! Be sure to visit Shane's website at http://shaneperez. blogspot.com, where you'll find all of the photos from that evening, along with an incredible gallery of nude photographs taken in a variety of abandoned industrial locations.

INTERVIEW WITH HOOT GIBSON

Next up is Hoot Gibson, of the recently infamous Hoot and Chief duo. These two seemingly came out of nowhere in 2010 and shocked the WDW fan community with their blog at http://mesaverdetimes.blogspot. com, which features extraordinary stories of off-limits explorations of Horizons, the much-loved EPCOT ride that was torn down in late 1999 to make way for the much-maligned Mission: Space.

I remember first finding out about Hoot and Chief when someone sent me a link of a static video taken from inside one of the sets from Horizons. Inside meaning, not from the Omnimover vehicle, but from a video camera that was obviously set on a tripod, filming from a perspective that riders would not be able to see from their vehicles. I assumed it was unearthed raw footage from a Disney-shot promo video, which was cool enough. But soon afterwards Hoot and Chief unleashed a ton of incredible behind-the-scenes videos, photos, and audio clips on their blog, and slowly but surely revealed the mind blowing story behind what I (and many others) believe

Hoot Gibson, molesting an Animatronic on the set of Horizons

to be a historically significant documentation of a now-extinct attraction.

Their often heart-pounding blog entries detailed paranoid and over-planned escapes from the Omnimovers, discoveries of hilarious props hidden by Cast Members in the sets (notably a giant black dildo in the Mesa Verde fridge), the secrets behind some of the best special effects in the ride, and cat-and-mouse chases between them and security guards through backstage areas. But most of all, the blog entries show an over-abiding love of an attraction that they knew was close to death, a thought which in their mind demanded action, risks be damned.

Hoot, introduce yourself and tell me a bit about your background and how you met Chief.

I grew up on the west coast of Florida so trips to WDW were frequent. I loved the place as much as any other kid but in 1976 the magnitude of it all finally hit me. I remember realizing that Walt Disney was a real man, he had talented men and women working for him, and REAL people created this amazing place. I wanted to be part of it.

When I graduated High School I packed my stuff and went to work at the Magic Kingdom. I applied to be a custodian because it seemed like the kind of job that would allow me the most freedom for exploration. I was right. Custodians are looked down upon by every other cast member and that's no secret. Most of them weren't very smart.....and I hate to say it.........but some were borderline retarded.

The incredible upside to the job became clear one night when I was on my way to explore the Jungle Cruise. I was making my way across the maintenance dock and POW a security guy came out of nowhere.

He asked me what I was doing back there and I said, "My Lead told me to come down here and empty a trash can but I can't find it." Security guy said, "Well that one looks like shit so empty that one." He left and I went on to sit on some Audio Animatronic elephants and photograph them inside and out.

Working at the park was far from what I thought it would be. The people there were mean and overall disenchanted with the place. I had imagined a place where I would work with the other fans of Walt Disney but it was far from that. My focus became more on gathering information and less on making a career. One crowded day on Main Street, a new guy showed up.

Chief walked onto the scene with his white uniform on and a book about Walt Disney under his arm. I said, "What are you? Some kind of Disney Freak?" He said, "Yep." I said, "Me, too." It was an electric moment for sure. We talked all day and come to find out we were on exactly the same page. That night we snuck into Jungle Cruise. The next night... the entire park. It started an amazing string of planned adventures that seemed to never end.

We eventually got fired from the Magic Kingdom. We didn't fit in so insubordination led to our predicted demise. I went to art school in 1987 and Chief joined me second year. We found that crazy shit happened wherever we went but the Magic Kingdom was still our focus.

Chief, posing with the Animatronic dive team in Horizons

On a basic level, what was it that drove you to explore these rides beyond the bounds of a normal guest? Most people are happy sitting in the ride, experiencing what they're meant to experience. Why did you need more?

We had to KNOW more. When we were custodians we asked about art and maintenance jobs and how we might work our way up to something like that. We were only met by smart assed answers from mean people.

I have a point to make about that. Chief and I didn't like being told we couldn't do something. Especially from those in charge of the place that we had dreamed about our entire lives. It put a sour taste in our mouths and gave us one hell of an inspiration to do whatever we pleased to get the info we wanted.

As a follow-up to that, this really is sort of an ultra-geek activity. You could have been hanging out at bars, picking up chicks, or playing sports, or whatever guys do in their spare time. What did your "normal" friends and family think about this? What did girls think about it?

We didn't really talk about our adventures with other people. I guess we thought that other people wouldn't care. Chicks thought we were stupid so we didn't bring it up. We had girlfriends but they never came along or cared about what we were doing unless they wanted to lay a guilt trip on us. I remember dumping a girl because she didn't know that there were two separate tracks to Mr Toads Wild Ride! I couldn't have that :)

It seems as if the Horizons exploration was very detailed and thorough, almost like a military operation. Describe the thought process that led up to it.

What makes the Horizons exploration special to us is that we had pretty much retired from our WDW exploits by then. Chief went off to the military, our third partner, who I can't name, got into a high speed chase with Disney security and was banned from property, and I fell in line and tried to make something of myself.

The closing of Horizons rekindled a deep feeling in me and Chief. It was an amazing piece of art that couldn't just slip away like some attractions before it. We decided to use the skills we had honed to preserve it all the best knew how. We did.

What made Horizons so special? Is there anything like it at WDW now?

There's nothing there like it now. I only go to the parks if I get in free and even then I don't even enjoy it.

Why did you decide, after so many years, to start telling the world about all of this through the Mesa Verde Times blog? It seems like you guys just came out of nowhere! For us Horizons fans it was akin to a Beatles fan finding out there were 4 unreleased Beatles studio albums hidden in a vault somewhere!

Hehe. My greatest fear is that I'll die and my pics and stuff will end up at the county landfill. I was flipping through my Horizons pics and for

Hoot floats in Zero-G with the Space Station family in Horizons

some reason I decided to blog about them. I didn't think anyone would care and neither did Chief. It became a way for the two of us to relive the adventure and we were happy as hell to find out that other Horizons fans are out there.

What has been the reaction to the stories you've published on the blogs? Have you been officially contacted by anyone at Disney with legal threats? Or has anyone in the company actually said they appreciate what you did? What about fan reaction?

We haven't heard from Disney legal officially. We really don't care what they think. They can't erase our memories and hopefully every Mesa Verde Times fan has saved our pics and writings. They're too late now and this is still America.

We have heard from several Imagineers, Pixar guys, and tons of WDW people who miss Horizons. We get hits from Burbank, Emeryville, Anaheim, Orlando, everyday. We hope they're inspired by Horizons and use the inspiration in their work.

During all of your WDW adventures, were you afraid of being caught and sent to jail, or worse, banned from WDW parks for life? If not, what was it that made you so confident that you could do this without getting noticed? Rumor is that every ride in WDW has a ton of hidden cameras…

There wasn't one time that we weren't afraid of getting caught or killed. Every Horizons trip was dangerous and we want to make that clear. I guess our will to learn outweighs our sense of self preservation :)

What are the weirdest/scariest/funniest things you found in all of your exploring around WDW?

Chief found Snow White's head in 1986 for no reason. We found a black rubber penis in the fridge in Horizons. We found a message from a friend while crawling around in the filth of Pirates of the Caribbean. We found condoms more than anything.

What advice would you give to someone who wanted to explore the rides today? Post 9/11, is it even still possible to do what you guys did?

Understand that you might die. Being caught is nothing but being killed is very real.

Years later, are you all proud of what you did? Any regrets?

Of course! We're totally proud. We regret that we didn't get to World of Motion before it closed :(

Any future explorations planned?

We're exploring right now :) Stay tuned.

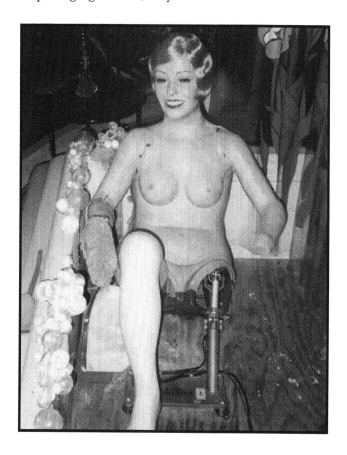

No, the breasts and nipples could not be seen from the ride vehicle!

Epilogue

So there you have it, a guide for a trip to Walt Disney World unlike any other you've taken before. Chances are you've been offended multiple times, shocked more than a few, and said "me gusta" more often than you'd care to admit. That sort of varied reaction goes to show that WDW is a place where people of all ages and backgrounds can enjoy themselves, however outside the norm their idea of a good time might be.

But let's make a solemn promise to maintain a code of ethics, a "do no harm" policy that upholds the right of every visitor to WDW to enjoy themselves, and to not have their vacation spoiled by those engaged in the "alternative" activities described in this book. By abiding by this code, we can best realize Walt's dream of an EPCOT-esque utopia, one where people of all creeds can live harmoniously together. WDW is vast enough in scope and imagination to accommodate that dream, and regardless of how much we fly outside the realm of conventional theme-park morality, we still have to respect the fact that a lot of other people have saved up a long time to experience their idea of utopia.

It should also go without saying that I don't advocate anyone engaging in illegal activities inside WDW. If you break the law and get caught, it's all on you. So before attempting anything in this book that might be potentially illegal, ask yourself, "Is the fun and excitement of participating in this illegal activity worth the potential negatives that would come with getting caught, landing in jail, and having a misdemeanor/felony charge on my record?" Obviously some of our interviewed subjects thought the risk/ reward ratio was well in their favor, and chose to engage in various illegal activities. But that doesn't mean that everyone has the same threshold, and if you're the father of three kids, living month-to-month, and working as a clergyman or some other such high-profile position, it might be best if you took a step back from those Utilidor entrances, refrained from using a one-hitter in The Haunted Mansion, and tried to keep your clothes on during that monorail ride from The Magic Kingdom to Epcot.

Well, that's enough from me for now. Feel free to follow my further escapades at the blog section of www.darksideofdisney.com. Since changes happen so frequently at WDW, there are parts of this book that might be out of date by the time it hits the presses, so the blog will also be where I'll call to light any significant changes to the parks that affect the tips, tricks, and scams referenced herein. The website will also be a perfect place for anyone to post their love letters or hate-filled diatribes about the content of the book for all the world to see. I'll do my best to respond to everyone in kind, unless you're just a total asshole, in which case I'll post a scathingly witty retort and then block you from ever posting on the site again. And if you love the book, I'm more than open to speaking at your event or acting as your own personal tour guide through the dark side of WDW... for the right price, of course.

So until we meet again, enjoy your debauchery-filled vacation at The Happiest Place on Earth!

Acknowledgements

I'd like to thank the following people, without whom this book wouldn't be possible:

- My wife, for dealing with and actually embracing my Disney obsession, and for designing the awesomely kick ass cover art.

- My good friends, McGeorge and Newmeyer, for their company, support, and courage during those tense early adventures where it seemed like we were always one step away from landing ourselves in DisJail.

- All of the WDW fanboy sites out there for providing a wealth of information, including but certainly not limited to mouseplanet. com, miceage.com, allears.net, wdwmagic.com, and disboards.com.

- Everyone who read the multiple revisions of this book, made comments and suggestions, and in some cases acted as full-on editors. Sorry I can't mention you all by name, but if I did the jig would be up with a quick FB search, and anonymity must be preserved at all costs to avoid the wrath of Disney Police and angry fanboys!

- Jonas Kyle-Sidell, for his excellent layout work. If anyone else out there needs a layout artist who does great work on a limited budget, Jonas is your man!

- Draven Star, our awesome and gorgeous cover model, and Alan Partlow, the talented photographer for that shoot. What a fun day that was!

- Justin Callaghan, creator of the "Florida Project" and "Waltograph" fonts, for making them available for commercial use at such an affordable price.

- Hoot Gibson, Shane Perez, Chris Mitchell, and my Cast Member friends, for taking the time to contribute to this book, asking for nothing in return except for the occasional handjob and/or bag of blow.

❤ And finally, my mother, for spending her hard-earned cash to spoil me and my sister with many, many trips to WDW, igniting a lifelong passion and thus (probably to her dismay) being the main reason this book exists.

Index

ABOUT THE AUTHOR

Leonard Kinsey was born and raised in Clearwater, FL, and was lucky enough to visit Walt Disney World over 100 times by age 18. As an adult he still harbors an unhealthy obsession with The Mouse, has acquired a large collection of vintage EPCOT Center memorabilia, and visits WDW at least once a year, maintaining connections throughout the rest of the year with Cast Members and other Orlando-based friends and relatives.

Kinsey has been involved in the world of media his whole adult life, winning a Pinellas County Cable Access TV award at age 16 for "Best Soundtrack" for a short film he directed and scored. From there Kinsey ran the television station at a prestigious university for four years, producing hundreds of hours of narrative, documentary, and live programming, including the genesis of THE DARK SIDE OF DISNEY, a 30-minute look at the off-limits areas of Walt Disney World. Kinsey then moved on to CNN International where he worked with foreign correspondents for two years as an audio engineer and robotic camera operator. Retiring from television, Kinsey now works as a Systems Administrator, maintaining server farms for one of the largest dot-coms in the world. In his spare time he has published a comic book and written and directed a horror/comedy film which received international distribution. He is also the guitarist in a rock band who appeared on a hit FOX show and released two internationally acclaimed CDs.

11046589R0

Made in the USA
Lexington, KY
06 September 2011